STRATEGIC
MOBILE
DESIGN
CREATING ENGAGING EXPERIENCES

Joseph Cartman and Richard Ting

New Riders | VOICES THAT MATTER™

Strategic Mobile Design: Creating Engaging Experiences
Joseph Cartman and Richard Ting

New Riders
1249 Eighth Street
Berkeley, CA 94710
510/524-2178
510/524-2221 (fax)

Find us on the Web at: www.newriders.com
To report errors, please send a note to errata@peachpit.com

New Riders is an imprint of Peachpit, a division of Pearson Education.

Project Editor: Michael J. Nolan
Development Editor: Box Twelve Communications, Inc.
Production Editor: Becky Winter
Copy Editor: Haig MacGregor
Proofreader: Darren Meiss
Compositor: Danielle Foster
Indexer: Julie Bess
Cover Design: RHDG
Interior Design: Mimi Heft, with Danielle Foster

ISBN 13: 978-0-321-58007-8
ISBN 10: 0-321-58007-9

9 8 7 6 5 4 3 2 1

Printed and bound in the United States of America

To my wife JiHyun and my parents for their continual support and patience.

—Joseph Cartman

To my wife Chloe and my daughter Leela for their saintly patience with me. To my father for always being the scholarly role model in my life.

—Richard Ting

Acknowledgments

I would like to thank Ricky, Anthony, Dorinda, Jeff, and Mark for the support of some great mobile initiatives. I would also like to thank all of the team members associated with these projects who put in the time to bring these projects to life. Without you, none of these projects would be possible.

—Joseph Cartman

I would like to thank R/GA and NYU ITP for opening up many doors for me and giving me the space and freedom to discover something that I deeply enjoy doing. I would also like to thank all of my clients that have trusted me to concept, create, and design experiences for their prized consumers. I do not take that responsibility lightly.

—Richard Ting

About the Authors

Joseph Cartman has over 10 years of experience in the digital space working with award-winning brands such as Nike, Volkswagen, Hummer, Saturn, Royal Caribbean, and Verizon. He has worked extensively on both the creative and developmental sides of the digital landscape and is fluent in bridging the gap between the two disciplines. His focus on emerging media has driven him to explore multiple channels from physical installation environments, to film/video, to motion graphics, to web, and mobile.

During Joseph's 7+ years on the Nike account, he has led multiple global initiatives focusing on the AsiaPac, EMEA, and America regions. His focus on Nike's performance and lifestyle categories immersed him in content development and artist/athlete collaborations. Joseph supported LeBron James in the digital space since his rookie year in the NBA, has been on tour with Kobe Bryant twice throughout Asia, has worked with the historic 2008 USA Basketball Team, and has directed multiple video shoots featuring Nike's top athletes. His projects have won multiple awards at AIGA, Andy's, Art Director's Club, Cannes, Clios, Communication Arts, and One Show. He has led multiple Nike mobile projects that utilize Flash Lite, J2ME, iPhone, IVR, mobile Internet, QR Codes, SMS/MMS, and streaming video technologies.

Joseph has a decade's worth of teaching experience and has taught numerous courses at the BFA and MFA levels at Parsons School of Design and Emerson College. His courses have focused on visual design, motion design, web development, video editing, and Flash programming—all with a strong concentration on progressive thinking.

Joseph is co-founder of the NYC-based creative studio Steady Ltd.

http://www.josephcartman.com
http://www.steadyltd.com

Richard Ting is VP & Executive Creative Director of R/GA's Mobile and Emerging Platforms Group. His current focus is on creating integrated interactive user experiences across the web, mobile, and physical space. In his 7+ years with R/GA, Richard has received almost every major industry award including the Cannes Titanium Lion, the Grand Clio, the International ANDY Awards GRANDY and the D&AD Black Pencil. During his time at R/GA, Richard has worked on key R/GA accounts such as Avaya, Nike, Nokia, T-Mobile, and Verizon Wireless.

Richard is a much sought after thought leader in the mobile and emerging platforms world having served as a juror for the 2008 International Clio awards, 2008 Webby Awards, and the 2008 Global Mobile Marketing Association Awards. Richard has spoken at numerous conferences for organizations and associations, including Advertising Week, the One Club, the Mobile Marketing Association, and Nokia World. In the past year, Richard has published articles in Advertising Age and AdWeek.

In addition to his commercial pursuits, Richard is an Adjunct Assistant Professor at NYU's Interactive Telecommunications Program and teaches the course "Designing for Emerging Media Platforms," a course focused on redefining the future of the digital music listening experience and the future of interactive TV on the web.

Richard himself was a graduate fellow at NYU's Interactive Telecommunications Program where his project work concentrated on systems design and mobile human computer interaction. His undergraduate work was done at Carnegie Mellon University, where he specialized in information decision systems and economics. Richard was born and raised in New York City and you can learn more about his interests on his blog.

 *http://www.flytip.com*

Contents

Introduction

The mobile landscape is an evolving ecosystem of constant exploration and progressive thinking. Mobile is more than just the device that we carry in our bag for phone calls and text messages with friends. It's a device that connects users to a wealth of information and portable experiences throughout the globe—experiences such as those found in art galleries, brand and marketing initiatives, broadcast and news channels, gaming, entertainment and sporting events, mapping, and much more.

And statistics show that mobile usage numbers are on the rise. With new handsets being released on the market featuring enhanced interfaces and functionality, users are becoming accustomed to new methods of interactive behavior or new features and are adopting mobile for more than just phone calls. As users become more fluent in the mobile landscape, they pave the way for developers to build upon past successes and failures.

Mobile projects require a strong creative strategy in which visual and technology play an equally important role. Designs are tailored for an audience based on accessibility, and the proper execution is matched accordingly. SMS/MMS, mobile Internet, IVR, Bluetooth, Java, Flash Lite, and 2D barcodes are all options. With over 5,000 handsets on the global mobile market, unchartered spaces in the mobile landscape present great potential for creators in this space.

Strategic Mobile Design: Creating Engaging Experiences is a book designed for anyone interested in exploring the mobile space. The book approaches the mobile landscape from an entry-level to intermediate-level knowledge base and is tailored for anyone in an academic or business environment who endeavors to learn more about the potential and application of mobile applications.

Readers learn the necessary core mobile concepts and approaches used to create engaging and immersive user experiences. Topics in the book include:

- Creative strategy for the mobile platform
- The mobile experience for a global audience
- Designing for a progressive medium
- Modes of communication
- Designing for your audience and their handsets
- Interaction design and visual design for mobile

The book features case studies of select mobile industry professionals who work within the mobile ecosystem on a daily basis. Each case study focuses on a different aspect of the mobile space and shows the application of the key concepts covered in the seven chapters.

All topics covered within the book are written from a real-world scenario and based on real project experience, illustrating the true potential of mobile and where its future is headed. The book's companion web site provides readers with additional reading and visual information. Up-to-date mobile projects and progress within the mobile field are also located on the web site. The corresponding web site is located at:

 www.StrategicMobileDesign.com

By the end of the book, readers should feel comfortable enough with the mobile landscape to pursue their interests in more defined areas, such as concepting, interaction design, visual design, and development.

Many of the same tools and languages that are used in the web design field are also utilized in the mobile field: Adobe Photoshop, Adobe InDesign, Adobe Illustrator, Adobe Flash, Java, AJAX, XML, HTML, and so on. Visit www.peachpit.com for a catalog of books specifically devoted to these tools and languages.

Mobile is a powerful medium that is still a relatively untouched area for many brands and projects. Just as the web was a bit mysterious when it was first adopted by the general audience, mobile has a sense of mystery and intrigue to both its users and creators. Topics within this book uncover some of these mysteries and entice users to explore further. Don't be afraid to try something new. Don't be afraid to take a risk. With a medium so new and with so much potential, you should feel confident to explore this space to its fullest.

1

Creative Strategy for the Mobile Medium

For centuries, print—then later radio and television—dominated the media landscape, as consumers flocked to these mass mediums to satisfy their appetite for news, entertainment, and content. If you wanted to follow the results of a presidential campaign, get information about the local weather, read the latest sports editorial about your favorite team, or catch up on the most popular drama series, then more than likely you were getting it over the airwaves, printed newspaper, or printed magazine.

The medium was indeed the message, as these forms of mass communication were the most effective means to cast the widest net over a large group of people. It was lowest-common-denominator messaging for a lowest-common-denominator audience. Society as a whole was engendered to accept and rely on these one-way forms of communication via the traditional mediums.

Prior to the introduction of digital mediums, these traditional mediums were leveraged by successful organizations and individuals to build brands, report the news, disseminate information, and create entertaining one-way experiences. From a cost standpoint, it may have been expensive, but it was the most effective way of reaching as many people as possible. See **FIGURE 1.1**.

The Internet Emerges

Fast-forward to 1996, and the Internet as a digital medium is experiencing explosive growth, after previously being looked upon as a network used only by academics. Much of the growth could be attributed to the open nature of the Internet, the lack of central administration, and the ease at which content creators could create and upload content. According to Internet World Stats, in just over 12 years since the inception of the medium, over 1.4 billion people are currently using the Internet worldwide.

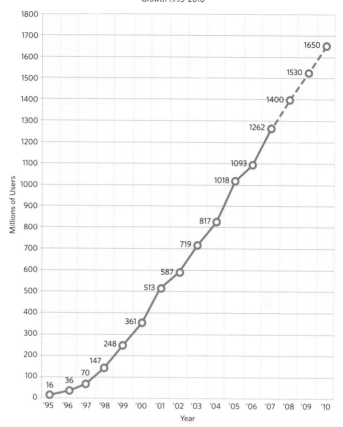

Explosive Growth of the Web as a Medium
Growth 1995–2010

FIGURE 1.1 The dominance of print and TV prior to the web and mobile. (www.internetworldstats.com/emarketing.htm)

The web as the third medium is now thriving as not only a legitimate destination for news, entertainment, and other forms of content, but also as a disruptive force to the "push model" of media consumption, which originated via traditional mediums. By utilizing a "pull model" for content, the web has begun to rival its two predecessor mediums for the hearts and eyeballs of users worldwide. See **FIGURE 1.2**.

Daily Personal Internet Usage
Home & Personal Time at Work

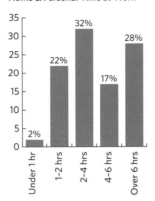

Daily Television Viewing

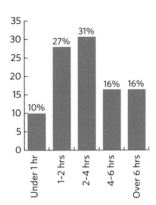

FIGURE 1.2 The growth of the web as a medium and the decrease in print and TV as the "go-to" mediums. (http://tinyurl.com/45okzt)

Digital Fragmentation of Media

In today's current media landscape, the web is officially recognized as the third medium. However, digital fragmentation is happening at breakneck speeds and has shaken up many brands, media companies, and entertainment companies alike. Marketers, interactive designers, creative storytellers, journalists, and media architects are all now faced with new challenges to devise new communication strategies, new modes of entertainment, and new forms of expression that leverage these emerging digital channels.

The technologies used by consumers to access content are changing. The old rules of communication are changing, with new techniques sprouting up across the digital landscape from web sites to viral videos to social media to Google Ads to interactive signage—and now to mobile, which arguably can be considered the fourth medium. But just as these new modes of digital communication become available, excessive content clutter is becoming the norm. See **FIGURE 1.3**. The signal-to-noise ratio of good digital content is unfortunately leaning more toward noise. This underscores the need for effective strategy, great creative, and pinpoint execution when diving into these emerging digital channels. During the course of this book, we will focus on mobile, the fourth medium, as one of these emerging digital channels, and help you effectively strategize, create, and execute for this exciting medium.

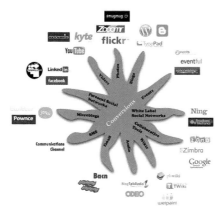

FIGURE 1.3 Robert Scoble's social media starfish.

The Mobile Medium Arrives

In just over 10 years, the mobile phone has gone from a voice-only device to one that can do it all—send text messages, surf the mobile web, download content, play games, play music, play videos, connect to high-speed networks, transfer media via Bluetooth, make mobile payments, and take and send pictures. The mobile device has completely evolved and has helped facilitate the convergence of multiple technologies into one singular device that is both "always on" and "always with you."

Mobile is the most dynamic and personal of them all, with unique characteristics not found in print, television, and the web, specifically location sensitivity.

A medium that originally started as a way to place phone calls has emerged as a platform for data consumption and social connectivity. According to the Mobile Marketing Association, *there will be more than 350 billion text messages sent in the U.S. in 2008, and that number is growing exponentially.* See **FIGURE 1.4**. The medium is as interactive as the web, where consumers can access the local news, watch videos streamed from their favorite video-sharing networks, and group-text-message their global network of friends.

Subscriber Connections

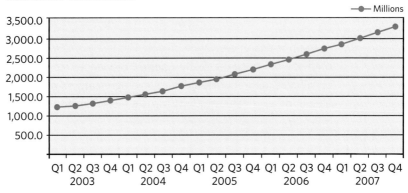

FIGURE 1.4 The growth in text messaging and mobile browsing. (GSM World, www.gsmworld.com/documents/20_year_factsheet.pdf)

Mobile Infrastructure Matures

As mobile matures and the infrastructure supporting it improves, we will see faster carrier networks worldwide, with upstream and downstream speeds comparable to PC-based broadband connections. Mobile phone resolutions are also improving, with some devices already supporting 640-pixel-wide screen resolutions. Mobile data service plans have also dropped significantly in price: Any average Joe these days can have unlimited mobile data access for as low as $19.99 per month.

Consumers now have access to better devices, with enhanced browsing capabilities; faster carrier speeds; and affordable, unlimited data plans. The stage is now set for the mobile medium to explode. These mini, multimedia-like computers connected to high-speed cellular networks and WiFi connections will encourage and help facilitate the ideation and development of next-generation applications, services, and creative expression for the medium. The PDA, mobile phone, MP3 player, laptop computer, and video player are converging into a single device. Simultaneously, rich media content—enhanced mobile browsing and native applications created in J2ME, Brew, Symbian, Flash Lite, and Cocoa—is now widely developed by content creators worldwide.

What Makes the Mobile Medium So Unique?

As mobile becomes a huge part of the media landscape, the medium will pose interesting design challenges, conceptual challenges, and opportunities to leverage features not available in other mediums. Short Message Service (SMS) usage has already reached a saturation point and has become a commodity. Mobile browsing and mobile content show the greatest potential for growth, especially with the integration of context-sensitive information.

The era of "always on, always with you" is upon us because of the mobile medium. To take advantage of it, designers and technologists must conceptualize ideas that leverage the following four factors:

- **Ubiquity:** Connecting to the Internet from anywhere and at any time.

- **Accessibility:** Accessing everything that is Internet based. You can pull information down or push information up to the Internet.

- **Connectivity:** Staying connected to your social circles at all times.

- **Location sensitivity:** Knowing where you are and serving up content based on where you are standing.

UBIQUITY

Regardless of whether you are sitting in the park at 3 p.m., waiting at a bus stop at 7 p.m., or driving through the countryside at 5 a.m., your mobile device can connect to the Internet (well, as long as you have a cellular connection). So if you have the urge to challenge someone across the globe to a multiplayer video game on your mobile device while waiting for the bus, now you can because of the ubiquity factor. If you need to access time-sensitive information while on the go, now you can. You no longer need to be tethered to a PC plugged into an Ethernet port. Nor are you required to be within earshot of a Wi-Fi hotspot to connect to the Internet. The freedom of ubiquity opens up many opportunities for designers and technologists to create new means of delivering information, entertainment, and experiences to consumers.

ACCESSIBILITY

Your mobile device has an always-on Internet connection capability. Whether the connection is a 2.5G network, a 3G network, or a Wi-Fi connection, your mobile device is now the equivalent of a PC that can always connect to the Internet. As a result, users have total accessibility to anything that lives and resides on the Internet. Database upon database of information, content, media, images, MP3s, and videos can now be accessed by your mobile device. If you want to blog via your mobile device about your latest vacation in Paris while sitting in a café, now you can. If you want to download the ingredients to the top favorite recipes from EpiToGo while strolling down the aisle at Whole Foods, now you can. The accessibility factor is driving the convergence between Web 2.0 and mobile and bringing the entire Internet experience to your mobile device.

CONNECTIVITY

By virtue of the fact that everyone's mobile devices are connected to the Internet at all times, you can share, discover, and stay connected to your social circles at all times. Existing web-based social networks like MySpace, Facebook, Flickr, YouTube, Bebo, and Twitter have already evolved and made themselves readily accessible via mobile. The connectivity factor is paving the way for interesting application features, such as sharing your music playlists, sharing your latest status feeds with friends, sharing pictures from your last vacation, getting product advice from your buddies while shopping, and finding out what everyone is doing on a Friday night. People want to be connected and online anytime, anywhere, and the mobile medium provides this.

LOCATION SENSITIVITY

Of all the factors listed here, location sensitivity is the one characteristic that is unique to mobile and unavailable to any of the other mediums. It is such an important characteristic that industry pundits predict that location-based services will play a vital part in the development of the mobile medium. When your mobile phone is turned on, users can be pinpointed immediately within 100 meters based on cell triangulation. However, more devices entering the marketplace are embedded with GPS chips, so the ability to pinpoint users will become even more accurate. As soon as users access a location-sensitive mobile application, it can answer these three fundamental questions:

1 Where is the user?

2 What points of interest are in the vicinity of the user?

3 How does the user get to where he or she needs to go?

By answering these three questions, a wide range of location-based applications can be created to help users with everything from buying movie tickets to comparison shopping to connecting with friends for a night out on the town.

Creative Strategy

Creative strategy in the mobile space relies heavily on the asynchronous model of concept, creative, and technology. Unlike other mediums, where stronger emphasis is at times placed in one discipline over another, mobile requires dedicated support from all three in order to function. See FIGURE 1.5.

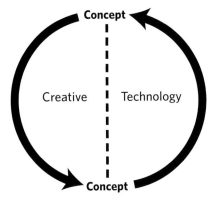

FIGURE 1.5 The creative strategy model.

Concept

Concepting, just like with other mediums, must not be driven by the creative or technology disciplines, but rather cared for by creative and technology. Due to the ever-evolving nature of the mobile landscape, concepts constantly challenge current mobile standards with the goal of exploration. This progressive thinking is what helps overcome current challenges and pushes the boundaries within this space.

Concept development needs to also strongly consider user behaviors. Different than traditional mediums, user behavior greatly impacts many factors of a mobile project. Who is the target audience? What is their mobile behavior? What is their handset of choice? What carriers are they on? Are they data-enabled users? All of these questions, plus more revolving around time, message, and place, strategically gear a project toward an audience. Any misinformation in this space will present a project that is not accessible to its suggested audience.

When researching an audience, concepts need to continually address how the project benefits them. For example:

- **Utility:** Is it a utility that consumers can use to fundamentally better their lives?

- **Art:** Is it an artistic piece that invokes a strong emotion or reaction in users?

- **Social communication:** Is it a communication component that lives within a social-networking context?

- **Controller:** Is it a project where the mobile piece functions as a controller and the payoff is in another medium?

Unique interactive experiences that include an element of surprise in their delivery are the ones that attract users and remain the most memorable, while well-composed utilities assist with daily life, such as banking.

Creative

Creative, which acts as the second component in the creative strategy model, refers to both interaction and visual design. Interaction design is responsible for determining the user flow, constructing the interface, and projecting the flow of information. Visual design refers to the skin that is placed upon the interaction design.

With mobile, the best visual design is clear and concise. Some of the best user interfaces (UIs) on mobile have taken six or more months to perfect, so mobile projects need to take cues from these UIs. Excessive visual direction can cause a screen to be illegible and also increase additional download time over a limited connection. Clear navigation is a primary area of focus for both interaction and visual design.

Creative also studies or considers how interaction will function on the various handset sizes (see **Figure 1.6**):

Figure 1.6 Multiple handset sizes.

- **Small:** 176 × 128
- **Medium:** 240 × 180
- **Large:** 320 × 240
- **Smart phone:** 320+

Technology

Technology, acting as the third component in the creative strategy mobile model, is what brings a concept to life. Based on an idea's direction, the creative outlet, and the targeted audience, the corresponding solution is decided upon. Such solutions include:

- SMS or MMS
- Mobile web sites
- Downloadable applications
- Rich technologies
- IVR

FIGURE 1.7 A sample SMS transaction.

SMS OR MMS

SMS or MMS make an idea the most accessible to a mass audience. However, in terms of promising an extensive experience, these technologies are the most limiting. Most mobile plans provide users with access to SMS or MMS. SMS is the transaction of a text message between mobile handsets. A single SMS transaction is limited to 160 alphanumeric characters. Anything over 160 characters is broken up into additional SMS transactions. SMS can be used in a variety of methods, ranging from standard communication to triggering or posting an event in another medium. See **FIGURE 1.7**.

MMS (Multimedia Message Service) is the transaction of a text-based message accompanied by a multimedia object, such as audio, image, rich text format, and/or video. MMS follows many of the same rules as SMS. MMS and SMS both require carrier approvals before they can be successfully deployed to the public. This approval process can add an additional two to six weeks to a project's development time.

FIGURE 1.8 A social-networking mobile web site.

MOBILE WEB SITES

Mobile web sites (see **FIGURE 1.8**) are another way to deliver a message to a mobile audience. In order to view a mobile web site, users must have a data-enabled phone plan and a handset capable of displaying such formats. With mobile web sites, a bigger breadth of content can be displayed and explored. Mobile web sites can also host additional multimedia components, such as audio or video. If user handsets can support these MIME types, users can access this additional content. Mobile web sites can also utilize preexisting APIs, such as mapping services, to enhance the experience.

DOWNLOADABLE APPLICATIONS

Downloadable applications, such as those created in Brew or Java (see **FIGURE 1.9**), are customized experiences produced for specific handset makes or models. These applications allow for a deeper, richer content, which can range from games, multimedia channels, and utilities to pure application-based systems such as banking. However, these types of applications require tailored configurations for each individual handset. Development in this space requires much research on its target audience's behaviors, handsets, and carriers. The application can be developed as a single piece of software, but additional development is necessary to port it over to other handset models. The development time for applications is much lengthier than mobile web site production.

FIGURE 1.9 A Java-based mobile game.

FIGURE 1.10 A Flash Lite mobile game.

RICH TECHNOLOGIES

Rich technologies, such as Flash Lite, allow for a unique mobile experience capable of incorporating animation, audio or video, and rich screen interaction. See **FIGURE 1.10**. Adobe Flash Lite software is a runtime engine that requires installation on users' handsets. This plug-in plays Flash Lite files, similar to the Flash plug-in for desktop browsing, but is developed for the mobile space. For users to interact with a Flash Lite experience, the plug-in must be installed on their handsets.

IVR (INTERACTIVE VOICE RESPONSE)

IVR is a phone technology that allows a computer to detect voice and touch tones using a normal phone call. Virtually anyone with a mobile device can interact with IVR via a phone touchpad. The IVR system can respond with a prerecorded or dynamically generated audio to further direct callers on how to proceed. See **Figure 1.11**. No special data plans are needed on the user end. This is the most compatible example of a mobile experience, where the end result lives in a different medium, whether it is audio, video, computer-based, signage-based, and so on.

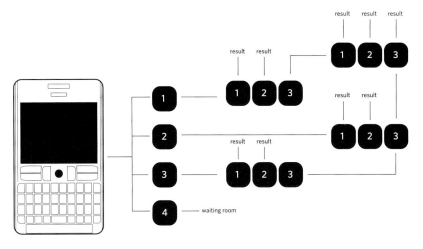

Figure 1.11 A sample IVR user flow.

Getting the User Engaged

Once the creative strategy has been established, the next task is to determine how to get users engaged quickly and easily with the mobile experience. Several methods can be applied based on the resulting mobile concept:

- Web-to-SMS push
- Text keyword to short code
- Bluecasting
- QR Code or Scan Code
- Mobile advertising

WEB-TO-SMS PUSH

In a Web-to-SMS-push scenario, users are exposed to the mobile project while in the online desktop environment. Here they are prompted with a form field to enter in their mobile numbers. Once they submit their numbers, users receive an SMS containing a URL to a corresponding mobile web site. The purpose of this technique is a courtesy, so that users don't need to type the URL on their handsets. A simple hypertext link embedded in the SMS provides the solution. In regions such as Japan, where email is primarily used on the handset, the information goes out via email instead. See Figure 1.12.

Figure 1.12
A Web-to-SMS-push scenario.

TEXT KEYWORD TO SHORT CODE

In a text-keyword-to-short-code example, a short code acts as a unique five-digit (or more) identifier code for users to submit a specific keyword to via SMS. Users then receive an SMS from the branded short code containing a link to the mobile space. The short code acts much like sending a text message to a friend, but in this case the submitted message goes to a service where a return SMS is dispersed back to users. See Figure 1.13.

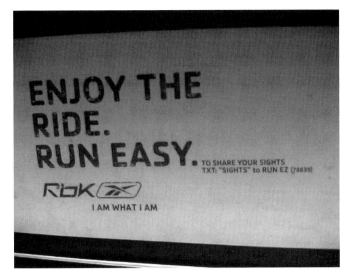

FIGURE 1.13 An Out of Home billboard that utilizes a short-code program.

BLUECASTING

Bluecasting is another way of transferring content to a mobile handset. Bluecasting uses a wireless protocol called Bluetooth, which provides a way to connect and exchange information between various electronic devices capable of supporting the Bluetooth protocol. If users have this support on their handsets, the transaction of data can only occur over short distances. See **FIGURE 1.14**.

FIGURE 1.14 A sample Bluecasting setup.

QR (QUICK RESPONSE) CODES AND SCAN CODES

QR Codes are a common form of mobile messaging in select Asia Pacific countries, such as Japan. A QR Code is a two-dimensional code that allows its content to be decoded at a high speed, typically via a camera phone. Data embedded in the code may contain a URL, text message, or general information. QR Codes originated in Japan but have extended into other countries, such as China and Korea. A similar form of QR Code, called a Scan Code, is also widely used in the Philippines. Users must have the decoder installed on their phones in order to interact with this technology. See **FIGURE 1.15**.

MOBILE ADVERTISING

Mobile advertising can play an additional role in increasing traffic to a mobile experience. Much like how banners work on desktop web sites, banners can be placed in corresponding mobile spaces to bring traffic to another mobile experience. Because the mobile Internet is still growing, users are curious to explore this space. Mobile banner placement can assist with this exploration.

With each approach, one needs to remember that mobile is a very personal medium; users have their mobile devices with them a majority of the time. Courtesy is the utmost priority when thinking through a concept and how to message it in the mobile space. To illustrate a simple scenario: Excessive incoming SMS is similar to receiving telemarketing phone calls during a meal. This scenario is not only disruptive, but also often eats into users' data plans. If the goal is to gain users with a project, this is a quick way to lose them.

Time, Message, Place

Time, message, and place help to determine what technology to use. Once a technology is decided upon, a list of challenges are presented in terms of what variables need to be accommodated for within those areas:

- Carriers
- Location or coverage
- Target audience penetration
- Adoption rates
- Localized

Variables represented in carriers need to be accommodated when planning a project strategy. Select carriers prevent downloads, so if a project requires an installed application that needs to be downloaded, individuals from your target audience may not be able to participate. With new laws governing the communication field, users must also be of a certain age to engage with commercial-based content. Carriers may also block specific technologies from their handsets, such as streaming, Java, and items that require unique installations.

If the project is more of an installation art piece, and Bluetooth is used, a focus on Bluetooth accessibility must be examined. What percentage of the users attending the installation will have Bluetooth-enabled phones? Is the outgoing signal within distance of visitors? Is there an alternative method of engagement that users can take advantage of if Bluetooth is not available on their handsets?

Handsets themselves present a wide range of variables to accommodate. Memory and disc space become issues for heavier applications. Not all handsets support the same audio or video or streaming CODECS. In conjunction with the carriers, users must have data plans enabled in order to access any online-based content. Smaller screen sizes may make a project more difficult to experience and navigate.

Understanding the penetration rate of a target audience and how these users navigate within the mobile space also plays a heavy role:

- Where do they engage with mobile?

- What are they doing with mobile?

- When are they using mobile the most?

- How do they interact with each other in the mobile space?

 Answering questions such as these will help determine the best approach in a strategy. Mobile media measurement tools, such as mMetrics (www.mmetricscom), provide intelligence on current mobile users, trends, and how they are engaging in this space. These statistics can be used as research while determining the best delivery format for a project.

 A preexisting creative strategy can be localized for multiple global regions. Translations can be implemented with a fair amount of ease, but the difference in handsets, carriers, and international standards poses additional work in the development of creative space. This can also greatly increase the scope or budget of a project. Even the smallest aspects of a project need to be thoroughly tested against a global model, either on the handsets themselves or by a service such as DeviceAnywhere (www.deviceanywhere.com).

Conclusion

The mobile landscape is rich in opportunity, with a variety of methods available to accommodate any project or target audience. Whether it is IVR, SMS, or MMS, mobile Internet, Bluetooth, mobile video, Java games, Flash Lite, or QR Codes, each has its own benefits in creating an exclusive experience unique to the mobile space. Project creators must be determined to push limits, explore new concepts, and think of new, invigorating ways to get users immersed in an experience. The need for compelling content must always act as the lead.

2

The Mobile Experience for a Global Audience

Global developments in technology and mobile strategies continue to push regional industries forward and progressively enhance mobile capabilities worldwide. GSM has become the world's leading standard, with well over 450 GSM operators functioning globally. These numbers continue to grow each year, providing a base foundation for the faster-speed-generation networks, such as 3G and beyond, which currently exist in major metropolitan cities.

From New York to Tokyo, how do mobile projects adapt to users' mobility within these environments? How do they add value to the physical context of the users' interests, their commutes, and/or their needs? What is the context in which they will engage with the mobile project? What is the speed in which they will engage with such content? With global business and global business travel, individuals have had more exposure to mobile content at an international level.

All cultures have different definitions of satisfaction in terms of interaction with mobile content. What is the acceptable method of delivery for a region? What is acceptable in terms of content? What is the voice of the content? How is the content delivered in a means that is not too advanced or too minimal? Is the content designed in a manner to reach a mass audience or more of a niche audience?

Developing global-based mobile content needs to address all of these questions.

Growth of the Global Mobile Internet

The mobile Internet has been around a little over 10 years, and statistics show that the global adoption rate has been fairly modest in terms of its growth. Growth in the Asia Pacific region has been much more aggressive than in the United States and Europe, partially due to population and demand. Only in these last few years has aggressive growth spread globally.

Even with recent data-enabled handsets that support 3G and WiFi, less than 50 percent of individuals with these handsets actually take advantage of these capabilities. However, adoption rates continue to grow, primarily due to three main determining factors:

- Handset manufacturer development
- Flat-rate data plans
- Applications and service development

Handset Manufacturer Development

Manufacturers continue to enhance their handset features and build phones designed for data usage on the go. These features include better battery life, screen dimensions, resolutions, and user interfaces. Viewing rich content becomes more of a simplified process. Progressive handset growth continues to increase users' interaction in the mobile space.

Flat-Rate Data Plans

As more mobile features are made available to consumers, networks are moving away from volume-based pricing and closer to flat-fee data pricing plans. This provides consumers with an expected bill at the end of each month, making them feel comfortable versus the unpredictable data plans that mobile carriers have often been criticized for in the past.

Applications and Service Development

Applications developed by Apple, Google (see FIGURE 2.1), Yahoo!, handset manufacturers, and mobile developers have taught users how to engage with their handsets, which stimulates adoption. Many of these applications become bundled in the handsets themselves, so users do not need to learn or download anything in order to use them. The more these applications are released over time, the more users become familiar with more complex interfaces and tasks within the small-screen environment. Application developers take cue points from the success or failures of applications; they don't reinvent the wheel with new application releases.

FIGURE 2.1 Google Maps for mobile.

The Growth of 3G in the Global Market

Carriers throughout a majority of the globe's metropolitan cities support 3G or WiFi access, allowing for quicker, constant access to content on enabled handsets. Faster connections provide fast, easy access to much richer content.

Core Growth Drivers for 3G

For the consumer, contributing factors of growth include:

- Multimedia and richer technology support (audio or image or video)
- Personalization and localization of services
- Streamlined data plans and expected costs

For carriers, contributing factors of growth include:

- New application development and exploration
- New revenue streams

For manufacturers, contributing factors of growth include:

- End-to-end solutions
- Operators need to fulfill coverage requirements of the regulator

Core Growth Challenges for 3G

For consumers, challenges that potentially hinder growth include:

- Full coverage and network interoperability

For carriers, challenges that potentially hinder growth include:

- Successful migration of existing customer base toward 3G
- New services to create customer demand
- Competitive growth

For manufacturers, challenges that potentially hinder growth include:

- Standardization of interface

The Global Mobile Community

One of most challenging aspects in global handset development is accommodating for the vast differences between regions. This not only affects the development technology but also development from interactive, visual, and communication standpoints. Not all regions interpret or receive content in the same manner.

From a technology standpoint, there are over 5,000 handset types available on the global market. Every country has its own set of carriers with their own governing laws and regulations. Much research needs to be performed, and a common denominator established, for a global project to hit the target audience.

The Americas

The Americas are composed of the United States, Canada, and Latin America. The mobile marketplace in North America is thriving with competition, while the Latin America market continues to rise. Increased mobile offerings, new capabilities, and accessibility to affordable mobile plans continue to grow in both markets.

NORTH AMERICA

In North America, the United States has a very progressive mobile market. With 50 states of coverage, each state has its set of carriers that are in regular competition with each other. Through competition, more and more handsets and networks evolve. Through this constant process, the American audience has been adapting to new methods of interactivity on the small screen. Users are data enabled and frequently engage in text messaging. Statistics show that users are actively engaging with mobile content, downloading applications, and are both excited and accepting of these changes.

The U.S. audience is currently experiencing 3G speeds in most metropolitan areas. With the vast majority of coverage in the United States, 3G is still not strong in rural areas, where speeds on the EDGE (Enhanced Data Rates for Global Evolution) network are much slower for roaming access, or for those who reside there. Data downloads and mobile Internet browsing are not as frequent in these areas due to the length of time it takes to download or view content. For those American users who engage with mobile content, they use it for email, weather information, news, and search options.

Although the United States appears to be advanced in regards to the vast quantity of handsets and carriers available on the market, this competition also poses growth limitations. On select carriers, downloads need to be served through the carrier for a fee, streaming media is restricted to certain networks, applet installation is limited to select handsets or carriers, as well as other variable network-dependent factors. Fifty states of coverage mean multiple laws and regulations surrounding mobile. Factors such as these make the quality assurance phase of any project rather in-depth. Users may have handsets on a select carrier that supports content properly, while a user on another network with the same handset might have difficulties with content.

LATIN AMERICA

The Latin American market has grown at a fairly steady pace since its inception. However, recently this growth has increased much more rapidly. Since 2003, mobile services and availability have increased throughout the region. This is primarily due to the costs associated with deploying fixed-line services and lines to establish these services in select countries. Due to the diversity of the geography, the population, and the deployment of technology, the mobile environment is diverse within the region itself.

Brazil, Mexico, Colombia, Argentina, Venezuela, Chile, and Peru account for over 50 percent of Latin America mobile subscribers. Currently over 375 million people own mobile devices, which is almost 12 percent of the population of the region. Mobile penetration is also considered six times that of the PC penetration within the region, with Brazil the fifth-biggest mobile market in the world. Users in Brazil are using the mobile Internet primarily for email, music, entertainment, games, and news or politics.

The current Latin America market share offers more plans and handsets, boosting competition on the market. However, the market is still primarily comprised of prepaid subscribers due to the impoverished population. Although users are prepaid subscribers, they're receiving services similar to users in North America.

Asia Pacific

The Asia Pacific region consists of China, Japan, Hong Kong, India, Korea, the Philippines, Taiwan, and Southeast Asia. With the vast population present in each of these locations, the adoption rate for new mobile behaviors has been growing at a much more rapid pace than anywhere else.

JAPAN

Mobile content is plentiful in Japan. Japan utilizes a higher-speed transmission protocol called W-CDMA (Wideband Code Division Multiple Access) and is part of the FOMA (Freedom of Mobile Multimedia Access), which was the world's first W-CDMA 3G service, launched in 2001. W-CDMA is considered a wideband spread-spectrum mobile air interface that utilizes the direct-sequence spread- spectrum method of asynchronous code division. It provides multiple access, allowing for higher speeds and support. Japan has no GSM network, so many western travelers experience inoperable phones when visiting the country.

Japan's mobile offerings, such as FeliCa and i-mode mobile data, take full advantage of FOMA services, making Japan a unique mobile country. FeliCa (Felicity Card) is a contactless RFID smart card system that Sony developed. It includes an integrated, nonvolatile memory and wireless communication chip that facilitates data exchange when held adjacent to compatible readers or writers. FeliCa is primarily used in electronic money cards, such as those used for mass public transit systems, employee IDs, and student IDs. The convenience that FeliCa brings to the consumer is increasing its adoption rate within the country.

For more information on Sony FeliCa, visit the Sony FeliCa global web site:

 www.sony.net/Products/felica/

Mobile consumers in Japan rely heavily on mobile-based email versus SMS or MMS communication. Handsets and handset software make email a desired preference of typed communication on the Japanese market. In attempts to limit the amount of spam within the country, Japan enforces strict laws against advertising initiatives, which prevent advertising contact with those younger than 13.

Japanese handsets take full advantage of the higher bandwidth in their software offerings. Many of the handsets support Flash Lite, where Flash-based content can be viewed on the handset via the Flash Lite player. Games are a popular form of Flash Lite–based content. They are simple interaction pieces that can help individuals spend time while on the subway, bus, or while waiting in line. See **Figure 2.2**. Software supporting streaming video and music is also more dominant in the Japanese mobile market, keeping users engaged with newscasts, music, and television broadcasts.

Figure 2.2
CharaJam.com allows users to design cell phone interfaces, greeting cards, screen-savers, clocks, calen-dars, Flash messages, and games.

2D barcodes, such as QR Codes, can be found incorporated in many of Japan's advertisements, subway stations, and store signage. Mobile handsets that support a QR Code reader allow users to scan the code with their handsets' cameras and gather relevant information on the images.

Japanese operators and handset manufacturers have worked together to ensure device support for visual-bar-code technol-ogy, which helps drive the adoption rate. Approximately 40 percent of consumers have used bar codes through their mobile devices. Consumers in Japan understand how to utilize the 2D bar code technology, whereas United States consumers still need to be educated in this space. Many times the QR Code in Japan is still viewed as a support gimmick, but in reality it provides immediate gratification for the curious viewer. Users are charged standard data rates, since the Japanese business model doesn't support mobile advertising.

SOUTH KOREA

South Korea's rich mobile landscape shares similarities with Japan in terms of its extensive mobile content offerings. South Korea handsets support Flash Lite, QR Codes, SMS, MMS, email, Java, and mobile Internet. The strong success of the gaming industry in South Korea has extended greatly into the mobile space. Flash Lite has become a software platform for this. Social-networking applications offer a means for the dense population to stay in contact with each other. South Korean handsets continually push the market forward in terms of their capabilities and network offerings, keeping South Korea's market one of the strongest in the world.

CHINA

The China mobile market has the greatest growth potential in the world. It has the world's largest market for wireless communication, with 20 percent of its market share in mobile networks. China has a 3G spectrum allocated for W-CDMA, TD-SCDMA, and CDMA2000. W-CDMA provides symmetric traffic for typical person-to-person communication, with an identical capacity for downlink and uplink. TD-SCDMA provides asymmetric data transmission for typical Internet sessions with a wide range of flexibility for download and uplink. CDMA2000 provides a hybrid version of 2.5G and 3G technologies.

China has over 500 million mobile subscribers, far surpassing the number of fixed-line subscribers. Operators rely on value-added services to attract their consumers, such as SMS, MMS, Java, games, IVR, and CRBT (Caller Ring Back Tone), as well as standard mobile offerings. Users in China use mobile primarily for entertainment, games, music, news or politics, and business or finance. Spamming is controlled in China and is not allowed on the networks. Operators take strict measures to enforce this rule. There is legal precedent in China of companies paying damages for unsolicited spam initiatives.

HONG KONG

Hong Kong represents a small city economy, with a population of over 6.9 million. The country has a very dense population and demonstrates quick adoption rates in the mobile space. The mobile market within the country is very competitive. Standard voice plans are relatively inexpensive, which makes SMS a more expensive comparison. Hong Kong was late in introducing interoperator SMS, which explains why its SMS usage lags far behind other Asian countries. Hong Kong users engage with mobile content, but they spend much more time with SMS and voice options.

TAIWAN

Taiwan has struggled with low mobile data revenues. Operators are aware of the need for interesting content and strong distribution channels. Recently, this has picked up greatly and has helped enhance mobile penetration, partially due to the availability of 3G and mobile number portability. With faster speeds, the ability to access mobile-based content is becoming more realistic in this region. Taiwan's numbers continue to rise as more initiatives appear in the mobile market.

PHILIPPINES

In the Philippines, consumers rely heavily on their mobile phones to access information online, more so than their desktop computers. It is also a much more affordable method in the Philippines's economy. Users engage with SMS, MMS, email, and mobile Internet to stay in contact with everything from news, sports, and entertainment. The Philippines also utilizes a 2D barcode system called Scancode, which is similar to QR Codes but requires a different reader.

INDIA

India has the lowest mobile Internet penetration rate amongst its population in the Asia Pacific region. Users in India that engage in mobile content rely on mobile for entertainment purposes, such as gaming, email, entertainment, music, and sports. Expensive data plans prevent strong adoption in the region.

India has also become a strong source of mobile development, where global companies are outsourcing their development tasks, such as porting, to India. India's tech industry has the knowledge base, and the project tasks can be achieved at a relatively inexpensive cost.

Mobile in EMEA

The mobile landscape in EMEA (Europe, Middle East, and Africa) is quite similar to that of North America. Email, weather, news, and search are amongst the top categories for EMEA mobile users. EMEA users engage with SMS or MMS, mobile Internet, Java, and IVR.

Compared to the United States, EMEA has significantly fewer carriers operating per country—some countries with only a small handful. EMEA's mobile audience is quicker to adapt to new interactive methods partially due to this factor. With fewer carriers available, both mobile offerings and handset development are consistent. Lesser variants need to be accommodated for as handsets hit the market. User knowledge is constantly growing with these enhancements, and that means users are better able to understand a variety of networks. The EMEA consumer adoption rate grows faster than the North American rate, where multiple carriers operate within each state.

The United Kingdom has one of the most developed mobile markets in Europe. Spain also contains one of Europe's largest mobile markets. Its growth can be attributed to increased competition amongst its carriers, which has brought costs down for the consumers. Germany, Italy, France, Austria, and Portugal are also actively participating in the mobile space.

Different than in the Americas, but similar to the Asia Pacific region, Flash Lite and 2D barcode projects will occasionally arise in the EMEA market. Select handsets released in EMEA can support these types of projects when set up with the appropriate software. Many times these types of projects are associated with mapping and city navigation.

For instance, in France, the Paris transport system launched an interactive campaign using 2D codes. Passengers can scan their codes to see when the next bus or subway will arrive. Passengers who don't have the software can download the application via MMS or mobile Internet. Mobile video broadcasts are also offered up throughout the EMEA region, where users can view news, sports, and entertainment channels while on the go. As seen in the Americas, only a percentage of the general audience has access to rich-media content such as audio and video. Handsets that support mobile broadcasting require unlimited data plans and faster-speed connections such as 3G. Areas in Europe outside of major metropolitan cities typically fall short of the faster-speed connections necessary to allow for smooth playback, similar to the situation in many rural areas of North America, while users within the major metropolitan cities throughout EMEA can take more advantage of this offering.

With the vast size of EMEA and the numerous countries grouped in this region, residents are often communicating with friends across borders. Mobile numbers between countries vary in length depending on the location. Any mobile projects that entail SMS need to take this into consideration. Error-checking code, which is typically in place for SMS forms, must not just check the length of the number, but also correspond it to the country where it is going. This will help determine success or failure in the send.

Developing a Global Mobile Strategy

Developing a global mobile strategy can be a complicated task filled with many challenges, but it's not an impossible one. Follow these steps to ensure all regions targeted within the project are accommodated for in your global mobile strategy:

1 Gather research and statistics.

2 Establish architecture and development.

3 Design for your audience.

4 Use rigorous quality assurance processes.

5 Manage global messaging components.

6 Manage regional costs.

1. Gather Research and Statistics

The first and foremost step in this process is gathering the necessary regional research and statistics. Find out how the individuals within the targeted regions are interacting and where they are interacting with mobile content.

With the vast majority of manufacturers, carriers, laws, and regulations constantly evolving in all regions, the most reliable source for region-specific statistics or research is to develop a partnership with a local mobile vendor. Local mobile vendors can speak truly to the local challenges at hand from real world experience versus speculation derived from industry statistics. They can speak to their most recent projects, where statistics can become outdated quickly in the evolving global mobile space. Local vendors work daily within region-specific regulations and often understand how to succeed with challenges where statistics may say it is not possible.

The second source for additional market research are from the reporting suites themselves (such as those provided by mMetrics, Forrester, Nielsen, and so on). Numbers returned from these reporting suites can help break down the population and balance it against the feedback received from the local vendor experience. Mixed with the real experiences of the local vendors, these reports can assure the right strategy for the project.

2. Establish Architecture and Development

Global mobile projects pose very specific needs and goals. With over 5,000 handset types in the global market, it is important to narrow down how the project idea is to be executed to reach the target audience. Typically the top 25 handsets are focused upon for "each participating country" with the knowledge that the manufacturers, carriers, and laws will differ for each country. Once the top 25 handsets of each country are selected, you must determine if these handsets can support the demands of the project's initiative and approach.

If the project is a mobile application, the application will need to be reengineered specifically for each handset, greatly increasing both the development cost and timeframe. For SMS-based projects, the short code needs to be established and configured for each country. If it is a mobile site, the site needs to be flexible enough to scale out across thousands of handset types worldwide.

Whether it's a mobile site, application, and/or an SMS campaign, the base architecture and developmental files need to remain constant. The incoming dynamic data needs to be the only variable information contained within the build.

For example, if the project is a mobile site, the actual project files must be the same set of files shared amongst all the regions or countries. However, the incoming XML files must be separated and served up for each unique instance. This means there is only one set of core development files, and the content itself remains dynamic. This safely allows for translations and core navigational content to be controlled via XML, thus providing a flexible solution to a complicated task. With a centralized code, base fixes need only be applied in one location, as opposed to multiple file locations. This makes the development task much simpler once the core architecture has been established.

3. Design for Your Audience

When creating a global interface, design takes into consideration the way in which the global community perceives interactive content. How does the project's global audience respond to certain interactive cue points and layouts? Is it too complicated? Is it too simple or outdated? Is everything for the region accommodated for in terms of project components within that design? Does it fulfill users' expectations?

Since all text within the project will be translated, keep all language-specific text outside of any graphical-based elements. When designing the mobile interface, most textual-based elements need to remain in system text so that they can be controlled dynamically via XML. The designs must accommodate enough positive or negative space for the variable word lengths that arise from translations. For example, text written in German or Chinese is typically 1.5 times the length of English, and that can make a fairly large difference in the small-screen environment. The translated text should cleanly print; if the text does need to wrap, the wrapping will be accommodated for in a clean fashion.

You need to accommodate for any country-specific content or buttons that may be turned on or off via the XML. For example, if China requires three buttons on the screen and Taiwan requires only two, the visual layout must safely accommodate for these variants. The same concept is true of navigational elements and content blocks.

4. Use Rigorous Quality Assurance Processes

DeviceAnywhere is the source for user experience management for the mobile industry: www.deviceanywhere.com/

Global-based project builds must go through a rigorous quality assurance process. The project needs to be tested on the handsets themselves and also using services such as DeviceAnywhere. Partnering up with regional mobile vendors for quality assurance purposes is the most assured approach toward perfecting the build. The project will also need to be viewed from a translation standpoint, in addition to screen layout and interactivity.

If the project happens to be a mobile web project, this process can be streamlined. However, if the project is a mobile application, the quality assurance phase can take much longer. With a mobile application, each application is uniquely ported for each individual handset. During the testing phase, errors are logged and the application is then adjusted accordingly, reinstalled, and retested. This can become a rather cumbersome process that not only takes an excess amount of dedicated time, but also accrues extra costs in the process.

5. Manage Global Messaging Components

When a global project contains an SMS component, a short code will need to be established for each country the program takes place in. Even if a brand already owns its own vanity short code for one country, it will be required to purchase and/or rent individual short codes for all of the countries participating in the campaign. The short code acts uniquely on the carriers that it is established on. The same short code may exist in another country, but it may already be dedicated to an entirely different brand or campaign.

The addition of the country-specific short codes brings incremental costs to a project. The country-specific short codes need to be rented or purchased separately, set up separately with keywords, approved by the country-specific carrier(s), and maintained or tracked separately. Partnering with a mobile vendor in each of the targeted countries is one of the best ways to streamline this process. Not only can the local vendors assist with this process, but they may also have programs in place that can help accelerate the approval process in a more streamlined fashion—thus reducing overall cost and time.

Japan also presents a unique variable in this mix, as it uses email as its main form of mobile messaging, which renders SMS unusable.

6. Manage Regional Costs

When designing against the variables present in global mobile projects, the phrase "Keep It Simple" remains a priority. Heavier page loads can often translate as heavier mobile bills at the end of the month. With the wide range of data plans and data transfer speeds present on the international market, providing a mobile build that is courteous to all its users helps maintain the project's success.

The five basic steps to minimizing page weight include:

- Organize the content in a streamlined fashion. Place the anticipated heavier-trafficked areas at the top of the page.
- Limit core navigation to five items or less.
- Limit page depth to three to five pages.
- Maintain good compression standards on all multimedia components (audio or imagery or video).
- Maintain MIME types to match the audience handset needs.

Global Mobile and Advertising

Across the globe, mobile can be found integrated with other mainstream media channels and spaces. These areas include sporting events, outdoor signage, magazine advertisements, television broadcasts, online experiences, and so on. Mobile provides the extra channel that is always there for users to gain additional information regarding an item of interest, no matter the location.

Mobile has changed advertising and the way in which it lives with consumers. Mobile allows advertisement to produce instant gratification with consumers, no matter the location of that consumer. In the past, advertisements or articles of interest had to be more descriptive. Now they can tease the consumer a bit more, which encourages consumers to explore in other channels. Location no longer becomes a question, as users can access content anywhere via mobile. Mobile advertising placed in subways, trains, and embedded in mobile sites promotes content across the globe. With those regions that support a larger adoption rate, more unique mobile experiences can be presented as options.

Contests have always played a big role in this space. Product giveaways, coupons, and free tickets to events are examples of how to tease consumers to further explore an experience. The handset is always accessible, and users don't lose anything by exploring further.

Global Media Content

Heavy media types such as audio or video were adapted in Asia's mobile space well before anywhere else. In Asia, handsets were already streaming network broadcasts, recaps, and music videos before those in the Americas and EMEA could access that type of information.

These media types are now widely supported across the globe. Better data plans allow users to feel comfortable accessing content without a large mobile bill. Users are downloading directly to their handsets, sharing with friends, and/or syncing directly with their desktops. Multimedia support originally started with ringtones, but handsets now represent more of a portable multimedia player than mobile phones.

User-generated content is also on the rise. As originally seen in the Asia Pacific region, and in early experimentations with mobile carriers in the Americas and EMEA, users are participating in more community-based content portals. Whether this content is in the form of photographs and/or videos captured, it's making its way onto the Internet—both desktop and mobile versions. News sites are beginning to rely on additional user-generated content to provide a live lens into recent happenings. Community-based blogging software has also become advanced, empowering users to directly upload or write from their handsets to their web sites. iPhone applications, such as the blogging application WordPress, allow users to directly blog from their handsets. Not only does this push the mobile field and train users to interact with their handsets more, it pushes the multichannel approach toward content generation.

Conclusion

Progressive thinking and development toward mobile content shapes the global mobile landscape. New approaches and experimentation are necessary for evolution to take place. As the global mobile community continues to adapt new ways of interaction, it opens doors to new levels of experiences and presentation of content. Manufacturers are continually improving their products to support the needs of the consumer, as well as opening new areas for developers. Mobile penetration numbers are increasing by the day, with more users utilizing the data side of their handsets. To keep these numbers growing, developers must come to the table with strong concepts that better serve users in everyday life.

3

Designing for a Progressive Medium

FIGURE 3.1 1980s-era brick cell phone FY8850 (voice-only mobile).

Mobile is a medium that won't stand still and refuses to be pigeonholed. As a medium, it has constantly evolved over the last decade and has been reinvented in ways never imagined. Mobile started as a medium for voice calls (see **FIGURE 3.1**), then branched out to include text messaging, web access, robust native applications, location-based awareness, and rich social networking. It now serves as a platform for multidevice convergence. Your mobile device is now your camera, MP3 player, email tool, and calendar all rolled up into one device.

On top of that, users can now utilize their mobile devices to connect with and control digital signage. Mobile devices can now also perform intense database querying and dynamic content generation, actions that were until recently reserved mainly for the PC-based web. Now mobile is a medium fast becoming as robust as the web, and starting to challenge it for the hearts, minds, and attention of global consumers.

Given the mobile medium's progressive nature, creatives, designers, and developers need to think progressively about what users will want to do on their mobile devices. We have only begun to scratch the surface with regards to what types of experiences can be pushed onto mobile devices. Standard learned user behaviors on mobile devices remain in flux: Within a short time span, standard learned user behaviors have shifted from simple phone calls to text messaging, taking photographs, listening to music, and surfing the mobile web—even to watching live television. See **FIGURE 3.2**. As handset manufacturers continue to pack in more convergent functionality onto mobile devices, the definition of these standard behaviors will continue to evolve.

Figure 3.2 Nokia N92 streaming live broadcast TV.

In this chapter, we'll cover the following factors that make the mobile medium progressive:

- Utilizing a mobile phone in unexpected ways
- Leveling the playing field for Internet access
- Bringing traditionally static mediums to life
- Utilizing mobile for more than just marketing
- The rise of service and utility, mobile experiences that matter

Utilizing Mobile In Unexpected Ways

From powering the world's first SMS political uprising in the Philippines to enabling Interactive TV to controlling a 23-story digital billboard in Times Square to using your mobile device as a credit card, the mobile medium is constantly being utilized in ways never imagined. Mobile devices started as a medium for voice communication and have quickly evolved in unique ways outside of their intended purpose.

Creating Political Uprisings

SMS has a long history of political utilization. In 2001, former Philippines president Joseph Estrada was forced to resign. Reports indicate that the opposition movement to his presidency was largely organized and coordinated with SMS text messages. In addition, in the 2004 Philippines presidential elections, SMS became a popular method for campaigning for or against the candidates.

SMS has been so popular and such an effective means of influencing political outcomes that the Islamic Republic of Iran actually disabled its nationwide SMS network during the 2005 presidential elections. Mahmoud Ahmadinejad was eventually elected president. Disabling the nationwide SMS network was likely a preemptive strike to squash any future political uprisings.

Enabling Interactive TV

FIGURE 3.3 *American Idol* voting via SMS.

Beyond its role in political revolutions, mobile devices have been utilized in other unintended ways. The next example is the mobile device being used as the main access point into Interactive TV.

AT&T and *American Idol*, the most popular show on television, allowed their viewers to text in their votes for their favorite contestants. See **FIGURE 3.3**. AT&T reported that over 78 million text message votes were placed during the 2008 *American Idol* season.

Text messaging is used by an overwhelming majority of the mobile subscriber base, so anyone with a mobile phone can interact with the TV show. Since 2003, the text messaging service of *American Idol* has been widely embraced by viewers and cited as one of the main drivers for text messaging awareness across the U.S. Before the show, text messaging was still a nascent technology in the U.S. embraced by mainly a younger audience. Since then, text messaging has broken into the mainstream and is now almost on par with voice calls in terms of adoption.

Making Mobile Payments

Another area where the mobile device is providing unexpected functionality is mobile payments. NFC (Near Field Communications) payments via mobile devices are starting to take off, and the mobile wallet dream is inching closer to reality. Now consumers can use their mobile phones as a payment method for making purchases, accessing events, or even paying for public transportation by touching the phone to a reader. Despite initial concerns, consumers are starting to feel much more comfortable with the level of security provided by mobile payment providers.

FIGURE 3.4 Mastercard's mobile payment service.

Recently Visa announced a partnership with Google Android to launch a new mobile payment service. After years of false starts and misguided hopes for the mobile payments world, the partnership announcement between the two giants is a positive sign for the nascent mobile payments industry. The new mobile payment service will be a set of applications for Android, Google's new mobile operating system. Consumers can receive notifications about transactions on their bank accounts. Most importantly, Visa and Google are developing a payment service that will allow consumers to make mobile payments using their mobile devices like credit cards, by simply swiping them past reading devices. See **FIGURE 3.4**. In addition to Google, Visa is planning to announce a deal with Nokia and has aspirations to strike similar deals with all of the U.S. phone operators and other handset manufacturers.

Lots of Nokia handsets have integrated NFC chipsets. These chips allow a mobile phone to work like a payment card so consumers can swipe the phone during a purchase. There have been lots of trials abroad, since the NFC infrastructure is more advanced overseas, but the Visa/Google partnership bodes well for the U.S., which has always lagged behind the rest of the world in this area.

There are several fundamental hurdles that Visa still needs to overcome to make mobile payments widely adopted. The first is to get the service on as many platforms as possible; dealing with each of these phone companies could take years. Each wireless carrier and handset manufacturer needs to review and approve the service before it is loaded onto their devices. Additionally, all the handset manufacturers will need to revamp their devices to include the chips and other technology necessary to support mobile payments. Revamping mobile devices so that they can transmit contactless payments and function like contactless credit cards is a very difficult proposition.

Figure 3.5 Swiping a mobile device to pay for a transit fare.

However, the most difficult and important hurdle is working with retailers to revamp their infrastructure with new card readers to actually read and support contactless mobile payments. See **Figure 3.5**. Growing the pool of accepting merchants is the most important objective right now. The more merchants that accept contactless mobile payments, the better the service can become, and the more users can adopt it. These hurdles are the main reasons why mobile payments have not taken off specifically in the U.S.

Connecting to and Controlling Digital Billboards

Our world is one in which all devices and PCs are ubiquitously networked—your mobile device is connected to the Internet, the IVR (Interactive Voice Response) system that you are connecting to is connected to the Internet, and the digital billboard that you are viewing is connected to the Internet.

We find ourselves capable of designing and creating experiences where your mobile phone can connect to and control digital billboards in real time.

One of my favorite examples of an innovative use of mobile phones as a game controller for billboards is the MegaPhone project created by Jury Hahn, as part of her graduate studies at NYU's Interactive Telecommunications Program. According to her web site, Jury's goal with the MegaPhone project was to create multiplayer games based in public spaces, but with mobile phones as the controllers into the game experience. Not only did MegaPhone leverage mobile devices in a way not originally intended, it also helped us to rethink how media lives within the OOH (Out-of-Home) billboard world.

FIGURE 3.6 Calling in to MegaPhone to play.

The MegaPhone project was an IVR-controlled, real-time, multiplayer, interactive platform for big screens in public spaces. Anyone with a mobile device could use it as game controller. Players easily join into the multiplayer game by placing a call to the phone number displayed on the screen. See **FIGURE 3.6**. Once connected to the screen, players could control their game play by either using a voice or a keypad input. It's a simple interaction to control your game play, and the barriers to entry are minimal.

Leveling the Playing Field for Internet Access

The mobile phone in most developing countries is what the PC is to the United States. In most emerging markets, the mobile phone is the most widely used medium for Internet data access, and there is a huge opportunity to create content for these emerging markets. Mobile devices provide better data communications in third-world countries for users who bypass the Internet completely on the PC. The mobile medium can be the means to reach wider audiences, generate mass awareness, and gain mass adoption.

Larger percentages of mobile revenues from emerging markets are coming from mobile data usage as well, and the growth is *not* coming primarily from text messaging. Although most users are sending SMS messages, it's the basic data services that are driving the growth. In a good majority of developing countries, most mobile users have fewer high-speed broadband Internet options than other developed countries. So the majority of Internet users in emerging markets access the Internet via mobile browsers. It's almost ingrained in their local cultures that accessing the web on a mobile device is more acceptable than doing it on a big, clunky PC.

History is repeating itself, as users flock to mobile devices as a primary means of accessing the Internet, when accessing it via the PC is too cost-prohibitive or inconvenient. If we rewind back to 1999 and remember iMode, which was introduced in Japan by NTT DoCoMo, it quickly became one of the most successful mobile subscription services in the world for browsing online information and sending and receiving emails. However, for most of the users in Japan, iMode at the time was their *only* experience with Internet access. Internet access in Japan was too cost-prohibitive because users were charged for time spent online (at exorbitant local call rates). As a result, many Internet users in Japan completely bypassed the PC-based web in favor of the iMode mobile version of the Internet. At the height of iMode's dominance (1999), the U.S. had almost triple the number of online PC users as Japan.

To learn more about how research can affect your design thinking, check out Chapter 6, "Interaction Design."

Nokia's Jan Chipchase describes mobile as a potential "leapfrog" technology that can lead the way to connect the unconnected in emerging markets—places like Brazil, India, China, Indonesia, and Africa. In the future, everyone in these emerging markets will need to be connected. We're talking 6 billion people, 800 million of whom cannot read or write (so operating a mobile phone for this demographic is very tough). That creates a gigantic opportunity for designers and technologists to create and design valuable products and services for the illiterate. It is an interesting challenge to the design community. Jan Chipchase also speaks about the importance of conducting user research in these emerging markets to understand what products and services these users want. How do we help level the playing field with regards to Internet access via mobile devices? To those who want to dive deeper into this topic, we highly recommend Jan Chipchase's blog, entitled "Future Perfect," at www.janchipchase.com/.

Bringing Traditionally Static Mediums to Life

As all media rapidly becomes more and more digital, it only seems fit that traditionally static mediums like print and out of home (OOH) billboards start to embrace and leverage digital as well. These traditionally static mediums have long relied on telling a story or spreading a message with a combination of a short line of copy and a supporting visual graphic. The print and OOH worlds have started to utilize a wide range of mobile technologies to add deeper interactivity to the experience. Here are some examples of how mobile is reinvigorating formerly static print and OOH mediums:

- Text-message-enabling a billboard
- Utilizing RFID to customize billboard messages to specific consumers
- Employing IVR technology to make billboards controllable via mobile phone
- Enabling bus shelters to distribute content via Bluetooth
- Employing 2D barcodes (like Semacode and QR Codes) to push consumers to more content on their mobile devices

The ability to bring billboards to life is now possible in a number of different ways, as you will see in the upcoming examples.

Text-message-enabling a Billboard

FIGURE 3.7 Texting your vote to an OOH billboard.

Back in June 2007, BBC World ran some extremely thought-provoking billboard advertisements in New York City. The billboard advertisements were aimed at its growing audience in the U.S., with the underlying message that BBC World was serious about representing all sides of a story in its news coverage. The billboards essentially allowed passersby to vote on which side they represented on the controversial topics depicted in the billboard advertisements. See **FIGURE 3.7**. The SMS votes were instantly captured, tallied, and displayed on the billboard, thus making the billboard interactive in real time.

Billboards That Know Your Name

FIGURE 3.8 Personalized billboard messages enabled via RFID.

MINI USA recently ran a pilot advertising campaign in major cities across the U.S., where it gave select MINI Cooper owners the chance to get RFID keyfobs with preencoded custom messages. As these select owners drove their cars underneath MINI billboards, the RFID-encoded keyfobs alerted the billboards, causing them to light up with custom messages. See **FIGURE 3.8**. This campaign might not have been the most useful or valuable service, but the project does give us a glimpse into what is possible with the use of RFID-transmitting chips.

Controlling Billboards Using Mobile

FIGURE 3.9 Controlling NIKEiD in Times Square.

In 2005, NYC-based agency R/GA utilized an IVR system to allow passersby to control a 23-story interactive digital signage system in Times Square. See **FIGURE 3.9**. Users dialed into the digital signage system to connect to the enormous interactive billboard, and then used their mobile device keypads to design

NIKEiD sneakers. Each user had 60 seconds to design his or her shoe. Once the design session was over, a wallpaper of the shoe that the users just designed on the billboard was sent via SMS to the users' mobile phones.

Bluecasting Content

Bluecasting is a term used to describe the transmission of small, chunk-size digital media to Bluetooth-enabled mobile devices. The small, chunk-size digital media could be anything, such as advertisements, graphics, MP3s, mobile tickets, games, or mobile applications. Brands and advertisers have leveraged bluecasting to distribute branded content to consumers in public spaces, such as bus shelters, subway stations, and airport terminals. Most bluecasting billboards can transmit media within a range of 30 meters. Consumers first receive messages asking if they want to accept the media. If consumers accept, the media is delivered to their mobile devices free of charge.

FIGURE 3.10 The Mobistar Abribus bluecasting campaign in Belgium.

In **FIGURE 3.10**, Mobistar, a telecom operator in Belgium, utilized Bluetooth technology to run a proximity campaign for its Abribus campaign. For one week, Mobistar gave away (via bluecasting) a Christina Aguilera ringtone to anyone within 30 meters of an Abribus bus shelter. Mobistar's chief communication officer, Chris Van Roey, said, "Traditional mass communication must give way to new communication methods. This campaign illustrates the concept of interactive communication and is based on the principles of permission marketing."

Bringing a Static Print Ad to Life

Hyperlinking the physical world to the virtual world has been a topic of conversation for the past few years. Many designers and technologists have tried to do this already by utilizing

SMS call-to-action links that are printed on print ads and billboards. However, a new wave of 2D bar codes and image recognition standards are providing other options to designers and technologists interested in bringing static print ads to life. Among them are:

- Semacodes
- QR Codes
- SnapTell

SEMACODES

See Chapter 10, "Connecting the Physical with Virtual," for a profile on Stan Weichers, founder of Semapedia. Semacodes are a 2D-bar-code, data-matrix technology that encodes Internet URLs into tags that resemble barcodes. The tags are then de-encoded with mobile devices that have built-in cameras and compatible Semacode readers on the device. Once the tags are de-encoded into their corresponding Internet URLs, the URLs can be accessed via the mobile device's browser. Semacodes have already been placed on print ads, bus shelters, and OOH billboards to entice users to scan them in order to launch deeper, richer mobile web experiences.

In **FIGURE 3.11**, H&M incorporated Semacodes into their advertisements. When users scanned the Semacode tags with their mobile phones, they were directed to the H&M mobile web site, where they could purchase the goods in the advertisement.

FIGURE 3.11 H&M's Semacode shopping.

QUICK RESPONSE (QR) CODES

Quick Response (QR) codes are another variant of the 2D bar code. QR Codes are very common in Japan, and they are considered the two-dimensional bar code standard. Like Semacodes, QR Codes can store Internet URLs. QR Codes have been utilized in print ads and billboards. See **FIGURE 3.12**. Additionally, QR Codes can be utilized in just about any object that someone wants to link data to from the virtual world. Also, just like Semacodes, in order to de-encode the QR Code tag, users must have camera phones equipped with QR Code readers that de-encode the tags. Once the tags are de-encoded into their corresponding Internet URLs, the URL can be accessed via a mobile device's browser.

FIGURE 3.12 Northwest Airlines's QR Code billboard advertisement in Japan.

Image recognition–based technologies are another example of technologies that hyperlink the physical world to the virtual world. SnapTell utilizes image-recognition software and differs from 2D bar code standards like Semacode and QR Codes in that it does not embed URLs in the data matrix.

SNAPTELL

FIGURE 3.13 A SnapTell-enabled advertisement.

SnapTell (www.snaptell.com) offers technology that recognizes photos taken by mobile camera phones. In the example ad shown in **FIGURE 3.13**, users photograph an image of an advertisement for Gillette and text them from their mobile devices to the text address provided in the advertisement image (707070). The SnapTell service then performs image recognition on the emailed photos and responds to the users with a mobile web site page to sign up for a free sample of a Gillette product. The technology works effectively on photos taken with almost all camera phones and in all lighting conditions. The SnapTell technology has already been utilized in magazine print ads, outdoor billboards (see Figure 3.13), posters, product packaging, branded cans, bottles, and logos.

Mobile Is Not a Medium for Just Marketing

Mobile has barely scratched the surface of its full potential. If our memory serves us correctly, every year for the past four or five years, industry pundits have deemed it the "Year of Mobile," only to see their predictions never come to fruition. In the recent past, a bevy of factors helped stunt the growth of the mobile medium:

- The technology had still not caught up with the vision of the mobile utopia. Mobile phones were pitiful in their ability to allow for mobile web surfing, and to process and play back rich media.

- Cellular networks were painfully slow in delivering on the 3G promise.

- Consumers have been slow to consume mobile data, mainly because the overwhelming majority of mobile content pushed to users is marketing and advertising.

The industry has also taken a technology-first, consumer-second approach. See Chapter 6, "Interaction Design," to learn about putting consumers at the heart of your mobile creative concepting. That chapter reviews techniques, methods of interaction design, methods of prototyping, and how to factor in the needs and desires of consumers to bring about innovative design.

FIGURE 3.14 Examples of a useless wallpaper giveaway and a text-messaging alert program. This is not the future of mobile—not by a long shot.

Mobile needs to be recognized as a medium for not just marketing. Because the device is always with the consumer, brands and marketers have jumped on the bandwagon and employed traditional methods of outbound-push communications (as opposed to focusing on creating service and utility via mobile devices). Unfortunately, outbound marketing techniques and bad advertising have flooded the mobile medium with limited-value marketing tactics such as sweepstakes, wallpaper giveaways (see **FIGURE 3.14**), ringtone giveaways, and useless text messaging campaigns. Mobile is the most personal medium out there, so create something for users that makes their lives better, not something that adds to the noise of advertising clutter.

However, content creators have been slow to jump on this train. With limited content to choose from and a lack of advertising business models available to fund content creators, the medium has produced a limited amount of valuable or entertaining content to choose from during the last few years. However, the landscape is changing, technologies are progressing, and advertising models are starting to form. As a result, brands are starting to recognize that mobile must be a necessary part of their multichannel, converged digital ecosystem.

The Rise of Service and Utility, Mobile Experiences that Matter

In his book *Designing Interactions*, David Liddle shares the three stages of technology development, and how people interact with technology at each stage. The development of the mobile industry has mirrored this development path in recent years.

Stage One: The Enthusiast Stage

During the enthusiast stage, technology enthusiasts don't care if the technology is easy or hard to use because they are simply excited by it. We've seen this with the mobile medium for several years, as only early adopters and tech leaders embraced it. For the longest time, surfing the mobile web was a chore. It was slow and unresponsive: Downloading over-the-air (OTA) mobile applications was a cumbersome task.

Stage Two: The Professional Stage

During the professional stage, those who use the technology are often not those who buy it. Think of all the business professionals using Blackberry devices and all of the mobile industry professionals using their own products and services. Professionals used it because it was their business to use it. However, it was still one step away from mass adoption by consumers.

Stage Three: The Consumer Stage

During this stage, people are less interested in the technology itself; they are more interested in what the technology can do for them. However, over the past few years, those who created mobile experiences tended to focus more on the technology rather than on the experiences that consumers found interesting. The content for mobile was unappealing, and the interfaces were poorly designed. As a result, consumers stayed away. The only folks embracing the medium were the enthusiasts and professionals. Unfortunately, a medium cannot advance without mass adoption by consumers. We believe the mobile industry is starting to enter the consumer stage. As such, designers and technologists must create an experience founded in the users themselves—not the technology.

Users are not obligated to visit our mobile sites or download our mobile applications or opt in to our text-messaging programs—that's why the industry must refocus its design efforts to be more user-centric.

Mobile Experiences That Matter

This section includes a few examples of the next wave of mobile services, applications, and entertainment that actually matter.

GOOGLE SMS

Google SMS (see **Figure 3.15**) is a simple service that allows you to find out local business listings, sport scores, and stock quotes by simply text messaging your search query to 466453 ("GOOGLE" on most devices). Google then replies with a text message that shows you your results. So if you're looking for the address for Blue Ribbon Sushi in New York City, simply text "Blue Ribbon Sushi New York City" to 466453, and the service replies with the address and contact information for Blue Ribbon Sushi. The service is free from Google, but your mobile carrier might charge you for SMS usage.

Figure 3.15 Google's SMS service.

AMAZON'S TEXTBUYIT

FIGURE 3.16 Amazon's TextBuyIt SMS service.

Another simple SMS service is Amazon's TextBuyIt (see **FIGURE 3.16**), which allows you to text a product name to AMAZON (262966) and instantly receive a return SMS with product information and options to initiate a purchase. Just imagine yourself in a brick-and-mortar Barnes & Noble location, wanting to do a bit of comparison price shopping. With TextBuyIt, you can quickly and easily check prices directly from your mobile device—you no longer have to wait until you get in front of your PC at home.

NY TIMES REAL ESTATE

FIGURE 3.17 *The New York Times*'s Real Estate mobile service.

The *New York Times* has made it easy to search real estate listings and get property information while you're on the go directly from your mobile device. This service (see **FIGURE 3.17**) is especially handy for prospective home buyers when they're running between open houses. Instead of printing stacks of open-house listings from the web site, just point your mobile browser at http://m.nytimes.com/re and enter your property criteria (such as location and price) or find a specific property by listing ID.

AOL IPHONE MUSIC APP

The AOL iPhone Music App (see **FIGURE 3.18**), made in partnership with CBS Radio for the iPhone and iPod Touch, is brilliant. The service is free via Apple's App Store, and it brings mobile music discovery to the next level. As soon as you download the App, you pick your genre of music, then a list of radio stations from both the Internet and across the country is generated for you to select from. Once the music starts to play, you receive the artist's name and song title for every

track you play. Lots of satellite radio receivers already offer this, but you have to pay a subscription fee for that service.

As we move into the third stage of technology adoption for the mobile medium, consumers will demand tools, services, and applications that are as useful and valuable as the examples just presented.

Staying on Top of It

Mobile is the Swiss army knife of mediums, and it keeps designers and developers on their toes. So it's very important to know what technology advancements are happening, and which of those advancements are enjoying rapid consumer adoption.

FIGURE 3.18 The AOL iPhone Music App.

It is a constantly progressing medium, so to stay abreast of the latest news, we highly recommend the following sources of information, which track the latest trends in the mobile industry:

- IntoMobile (www.intomobile.com/)
- MobileMarketer (http://mobilemarketer.com/)
- FierceWireless (www.fiercewireless.com/)
- WirelessWeek (http://wirelessweek.com/)
- Mobile Entertainment (www.mobile-ent.biz/)
- mocoNews (www.moconews.net/)
- MobileCrunch (www.mobilecrunch.com/)

Conclusion

"Mobile devices have become indispensable in daily life. At the same time, such devices are advancing to offer connectivity to an ever greater number of things in the world around us, offering new benefits and convenience for leisure and business... It is a vision of a future world in which people communicate by conveying not only words, but also human warmth. A world where objects everywhere connect to offer ubiquitous access to a wealth of information and an array of useful services... It is not a dream that will be realized many generations later, but one that will come to life in the not-too-distant future."

—*NTT DoCoMo statement about the future of mobile*

Since mobile phones became consumer accessories in the mid-to-late '90s, the medium has evolved and morphed in many directions. As a result, the medium is looked upon as one of the more progressive mediums. Designers and technologists are constantly reinventing or reutilizing the mobile device in unexpected ways. Additionally, there are several emerging markets that use the mobile device as a leapfrog technology that will require an entirely different set of services and applications. Mobile devices can also serve as a way to bring traditional static mediums to life. Finally, the mobile device is no longer just a phone, but a convergence of many devices. With such a wide range of capabilities and features on the mobile device, it is important to remember that mobile is not just a medium for marketing and that in order for the medium to grow and evolve, we need to provide service and utility first and create mobile experiences that matter.

So when designing for this progressive medium, take risks to create and innovate the unexpected. Design experiences that are unique and useful. Enable consumers to fundamentally better their lives. Think message, time, and place. Lastly, create simple experiences that simply work.

4

Modes of
Communication

The success of a mobile campaign not only relies on the target audiences' mobile behaviors and usage trends, but also on the promotional visibility of the campaign and the audiences' exposure to the promotions. As with traditional media projects, mobile promotions need to be strategic in their delivery and incorporate their audiences' choice of environments.

Analyzing users' interactions within these additional spaces helps define the best mode of communication, or if the project needs to make use of all modes as part of a multichannel campaign. Examples of these modes of communication are:

1 Mobile to mobile

2 Web to mobile

3 OOH (Out of Home) or print to mobile

4 Broadcast to mobile

5 Radio to mobile

A true multichannel project considers and executes on all of these modes of communication. The project's message is then well represented in each channel; each channel supports the others with a unique experience and a cohesive theme exclusive to that channel.

With this model, the most important factor is that the content and approach in each channel must complement, not replicate, each other. Each channel's delivery has its own unique benefits that only that channel can provide. In addition, each channel must not be used just for the sake of using it—be smart in the strategy.

Integrating mobile into any traditional media campaign is extremely valuable, since users carry their mobile devices at nearly all times. Content placed in the mobile space can support traditional media content and create an extensive experience for the project, product, or brand. It can be used to answer any immediate questions that users have regarding content in the other channels, thus providing immediate gratification with the project.

Mobile to Mobile

Cross-promotion within the mobile space itself is a method that can help boost a project's presence for users already exploring the mobile space. The benefit of this approach is that it does not first have to draw users into the mobile space, in order to prompt them to experience the project. The task is just getting them to the content. These users understand mobile behavior and know how to navigate their way around.

Mobile Advertising Units

One method of promoting a project within the mobile space is through mobile banner units. Similar to regular online banners, mobile banners are placed on mobile sites or portals that serve related or corresponding content. Mobile banners are typically served as static images, since animations are not supported on most handsets. Since the images are static, these banners need to clearly illustrate what the project is in a very small dimension and also in a static state. The messaging within the banner itself needs to be written in a direct fashion, so that it clearly communicates where users will click-through to.

When the Internet first started attracting a global audience, users clicked on advertising units for the sake of seeing what else was out there. The mobile Internet is very similar: Users curious about mobile now click on mobile advertising units for the sake of exploration. These users may also not know how to search for specific content otherwise, so the banners actually help them. Companies can set up mobile advertising banners by purchasing a media buy, similar to how it works for online media. Mobile banner units help promote brands, organizations, and projects.

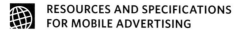

RESOURCES AND SPECIFICATIONS FOR MOBILE ADVERTISING

Here are some helpful resources and specifications for mobile advertising:

Mobile Applications

An educational white paper on the opportunities for mobile applications in mobile advertising.

http://mmaglobal.com/mobileapplications.pdf

Mobile Advertising Guidelines

Global mobile advertising formats and best practices for display and messaging.

http://mmaglobal.com/mobileadvertising.pdf

Mobile Advertising Overview

An educational white paper on the opportunities for mobile advertising.

http://mmaglobal.com/mobileadoverview.pdf

Crosslinking

Crosslinking content within the mobile space helps promote relevant content through preexisting mobile Internet sites. The more mobile Internet sites implement this strategy, the faster and bigger the mobile Internet space becomes. For example, if a site with sports content lives in the mobile space, it makes sense to provide additional links to mobile Internet content pertaining to relevant athletes, training, sport scores, products, tickets, or anything else pertaining to the sport. Since mobile Internet sites are typically small in size, this creates a much bigger experience for users to explore.

SMS

SMS is another way to promote mobile projects or content from within the mobile space. Forward-to-a-friend functionality empowers a user to input a friend's phone number into a mobile form field and SMS the mobile site's link to them. SMS/MMS functionality can also include links to additional exclusive content, applications, ringtones, and wallpaper. In addition, SMS opt-in functionality can be built into mobile sites, where users can opt-in for future SMS communication with the project, such as weather reports, news reports, sports scores, and so on. This constant communication must only be done if users have opted-in for the service. Spam must never be used as a means to promote anything, especially in the mobile space.

FIGURE 4.1 A live news feed.

Live Feeds

Integrating some variant of a live feed (see FIGURE 4.1) or an update component into a downloadable mobile application is a great way for users to stay included on all news- or update-related items. This is an efficient way to serve users content without asking them to engage in any additional steps on a daily basis. Once users have the application installed on their handsets, all content is sent to them. This technique can be applied to various applications and genres, such as world-news-related items, weather reports, and entertainment.

Network carriers and handset developers have teamed up to develop preinstalled system software for select devices. This software serves much like the live news feeds, but instead of streaming in text- or image-based data, users can also access streaming multimedia components. Since the software is preinstalled in the handset prior to purchase, the step of users downloading and installing applications is eliminated. This safely provides the general audience with access to rich content, thus increasing their knowledge of both the content and the mobile space. This approach also eliminates the need for users to take additional steps of locating content—it is served to them.

Web to Mobile

Promoting mobile from within the web sphere adds user convenience to the flow of any project. With available technologies and services in both spaces, a universal bridge can be formed to guide users along a path and set a direction for their experience. Since both worlds work in a nonlinear fashion, both spaces can strongly present interactive components that complement and feed off each other.

FIGURE 4.2 A web-to-SMS submission form.

Web to SMS

A web-to-SMS form can greatly assist in navigating users from the web space to the mobile space. The web-to-SMS form (see **FIGURE 4.2**) allows users to submit their phone numbers through an online web site form.

Once users submit their mobile numbers, they receive a corresponding SMS. This SMS-based interaction can be used in many ways:

- The SMS can contain a 160-character message pertaining to the project.

- The web-to-SMS form can contain an opt-in, so the SMS users receive is one of a series—for example, sports scores or weather reports.

- The SMS could contain a 160-character message that contains a link to a mobile Internet site. Once users click the link, they will be navigated over to the mobile site for a complementary experience.

- The SMS could also contain a link to download an application, such as a Java game or a Flash Lite.

- The SMS could contain a link to download a ringtone. When users click the link, the corresponding web server detects the device type and serves up the appropriate ringtone format for that device.

- The SMS could contain a link to download a video. When users click the link, the corresponding web server detects the device type and serves up the appropriate video format for that device.

- The SMS could contain a link to download wallpaper. When users click the link, the corresponding web server detects the device type and serves up the appropriate image dimension for that device.

With the previous scenarios and others, the corresponding mobile experience needs to always complement what happens within the digital space—not simply replicate it. The most impactful, memorable experiences are the ones that leave a sense of intrigue to be pursued in the mobile space. Developers need to also add disclaimers that users must have unlimited data plans for all mobile Internet packages. Otherwise, users may end up with a heavier bill.

Download and Sync

Online users can also encounter mobile downloads via web sites. These downloads can be applications, image galleries, videos, Flash Lite experiences, ringtones, and more. These experiences are bundled into the interaction design of the online web site. Users encounter a mobile section and are prompted to download content.

These downloaded applications can also contain a live feed from the web site. For example, a downloaded application that has been installed on the mobile device can also pull in updates or news from the main web site via RSS feeds. This feed can be anything relevant from news, sales, updates, or anything related to project genre. If it is a game, it can be additional levels, additional characters, or skins. If users download or install applications on their handsets, they will likely appreciate a feed.

Interactive Voice Response (IVR)

The integration of an IVR (Interactive Voice Response) element into the online environment has become a somewhat playful feature among many campaign and Hollywood movie web sites. See **Figure 4.3**. It extends the online web experience into the mobile space in an effort to push users to movie theatres.

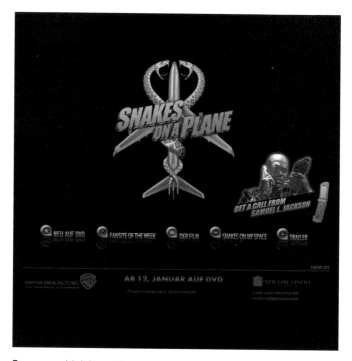

Figure 4.3 Mobile—Hollywood style.

With an IVR experience, users explore the online web site and interact with a "phone call creator." Through a series of set parameters and preselected lines of speech, users build the dialogue that the character is to speak. At the end of the interaction flow, users can preview the dialogue and then submit their friend's mobile number in order to send them the dialogue snippet as a prank.

Within minutes, the friend receives a call from the voice of the character from the web site. Projects that are more in-depth can actually personalize the name of the person who receives the call, so that the individual is addressed properly when he or she answers the phone. When stitched together, the dialogue appears somewhat real at first, providing a good laugh.

Out of Home (OOH) or Print to Mobile

Traditional advertising, such as print ads and Out of Home billboard advertisements, needs to be impactful enough to grab readers before they flip the page of a magazine. Color, type, and image all need to work together within microseconds of viewing. Once the advertisement gets readers' attention, they absorb the message and move on. If a traditional medium has mobile as an option, it allows the message or story to carry further and play out. The still image can now become motion or interactive. The mobile component can also satisfy any immediate questions or curiosity that users might have regarding content.

FIGURE 4.4 A print-to-mobile purchase.

SMS

With print and OOH, you need to implement an SMS component to best reach a target audience. With SMS, users don't need any special applications on their devices, nor do they need intensive data plans. A majority of the mass audience understands how to use SMS on their handsets, and readers who are interested will be more willing to participate in the campaign. See **FIGURE 4.4**.

The implementation of SMS into traditional advertisements can serve a series of functions. Here are some sample scenarios:

■ **Text the keyword "details" to 12345 to find out more.** Users receive a standard 160-character SMS with details pertaining to the print ad.

■ **Text the keyword "weather" to 12345 to sign up for weather alerts.** Users opt-in for communication of an SMS service, which disperses message alerts pertaining to weather. This could be applied to any other genres, such as news, sports, and so on.

- **Text the keyword "tickets" to 12345 for tickets.** Users receive an SMS containing an admission ticket number for the concert. If the concert is free, users show their ticket numbers at the door. If users need to purchase the concert tickets, they receive a PIN that reserves their tickets. They then enter their PIN online to complete the purchase on a web page that includes additional concert content.

- **Text the keyword "coupon" to 12345.** Users receive an SMS containing a mobile coupon. Users bring this coupon to the store for a special discount.

- **Text the keyword "go" to 12345 to learn more.** Users receive a standard 160-character SMS containing a link to the mobile Internet site. Any copy and the URL must fit within the 160-character limit. The mobile Internet site brings the print ad to life via interactive components and rich media downloads.

- **Text the keyword "game" to 12345 to download a game.** Users receive an SMS containing a link to download a mobile game. When users click the link, they're directed to a mobile URL that detects their handset type and tailors the applet to their handsets.

- **Text the keyword "music" to 12345 to download a music sample.** Users receive an SMS containing a link to download an artist's song. When users click the link, they're directed to a mobile URL that detects their handset type and downloads the appropriate audio format (MP3, WAV, or WMV).

- **Text the keyword "view" to 12345 to view a commercial.** Users receive an SMS containing a link to download and view a commercial. When users click the link, they're directed to a mobile URL that detects their handset type and downloads or streams the appropriate video format (MP4, 3GP, or WMV).

- **Text the keyword "wallpaper" to 12345 to download wallpaper.** Users receive an MMS containing the mobile wallpaper, and the wallpaper size is customized to fit their handsets because their handset types were detected with the orginal text message.

The call to action is very direct in all these scenarios. The keyword that users submit is short. Each keyword is tailored in the language of the campaign, and those keywords remain a single word only. Some users still use nine-button mobile devices, so keep keywords short to ensure a smooth interactive experience. The previous scenarios are also simple enough for users of all mobile levels to grasp.

Bluetooth and WiFi

FIGURE 4.5 A sample Bluetooth broadcasting station.

Traditional media that exists in store displays, bus shelters, and billboards are real-environment locations where a mobile transaction can occur. If a broadcasting station is set up within the structure, these advertisements can make use of Bluetooth and WiFi casting. See **FIGURE 4.5**. Users download content directly to their handsets per the directions in the advertisement. This is an immediate connection if users understand how to operate such technologies.

For example, users emerge from a subway station in a major metropolitan city. They pass by a subway billboard where they can "accept" a Bluetooth connection and receive a map of the local area. Once users sync with the sign, the application loads to their handsets. In another scenario, perhaps a subway stop in a district features an exciting nightlife that attracts a young crowd. A music label could market songs for that audience by offering ringtones or music in a billboard at or near that location's subway stop. In an art gallery, a mini interactive application can be given away to users within the gallery itself, as they view the current exhibits. This application can contain exclusive content unique to each exhibit, as well as an interactive component that might trigger a part of the exhibit if that part is a digital piece.

For these scenarios, users must have a Bluetooth- and/or WiFi-enabled handset. Users also must understand how to operate a Bluetooth connection (or the signage can provide step-by-step instructions). Once users receive the download-able item, they also need to know where to find and run the file on their devices.

Certain handsets also have limited storage space, so the applet must be developed in a manner where the file size is relatively small to accommodate a vast majority of handsets. Once the application has been developed, it needs to be ported in order to run on multiple variants of handsets. If the applet is not sup-ported across all handsets of the target audience, an alterna-tive experience must be served up, such as an SMS or mobile Internet portal to handle such alternative content.

IVR

IVR (Interactive Voice Response) can reach anybody with a mobile phone. No additional mobile knowledge or applications are needed. IVR does not need to rely on special handsets or carriers. Using IVR can complement any project that has sig-nificant content. IVR works much like an interactive phone call, where users call a number and they're greeted by a recording that provides a series of selections. Users make their selec-tions and listen to the recordings. IVR can be used for a variety of projects, such as learning about art installations, museums, entertainment, product campaigns, or even for making imme-diate purchases. Sample scenarios include:

- Users encounter a billboard outside a famous landmark. The billboard promotes a number to call for more informa-tion (for example, "Call 1-800-555-1212 to learn about this location"). When users call, they are prompted through a series of gateways on the phone and are presented with narratives about the significance of that particular loca-tion. Users can choose from a variety of gateways to tailor their experiences.

- At an art gallery, users encounter plaques located near each exhibit that provide a phone number to call for more information about each piece. When users call, they are presented with a series of gateways and are provided with descriptions based on their selections.

- Users encounter a billboard outside a concert hall where a musician has been performing. The sign provides a phone number to call to hear samples from the artist's latest album. When users call, they are prompted through a series of gateways. Based on which numbers they press, they hear samples of music tracks from the album.

IVR is a great way to create an impactful experience, especially if there is a recognizable voice associated with the project. This tends to deliver a more truthful experience to users and sometimes a more personal experience.

2D Barcodes (QR and Scancode)

In Asia, a 2D barcode (such as a QR Code or Scan Code) can be implemented into magazine advertisements, signage, product packaging, and subway signage. See FIGURE 4.6. The 2D barcode contains unique information pertaining to that content. If users have the reader on their phones, they can scan the code and utilize these options:

- Receive an immediate SMS or email with relevant information to the location of their scan. For instance, if the QR Code is present on a store display, users receive an incoming message that reads, "Present this coupon for 10 percent off today's purchase."

- Receive a URL sent to their mobile Internet browsers, where they can continue to explore benefits of the item of focus. For example, if the QR Code is present on a billboard or in a magazine, users receive incoming URLs from their scans that point to the product's mobile Internet site, where users receive additional details and downloadable items related to the product.

FIGURE 4.6 QR Code examples.

Users must have barcode readers installed on their handsets in order to engage with these experiences. There is a small market for this approach in EMEA, but in the Americas, few handsets support the technology and consumers don't fully understand how to utilize QR Codes. However, the barcode is a niche way to get attention on an advertisement, museum plaque, subway station, billboard, product display, or any other real-environment interactions.

Mobile Internet for Print

Many publications have slowly been turning to mobile and putting their content into the mobile space, so it's more easily accessible to users on the go. Promotion for these spaces takes place both in the print publications and the publications' associated web sites. Although print has always been portable, the benefits of print in a digital format allows users to access all of their daily reads from one location—the handset. They don't need to carry multiple papers. Users can also read up-to-the-minute news on the mobile Internet; with print news, users must wait for the next printing.

Broadcast to Mobile

As mobile penetration has continued to increase in recent years, so has the growth of handset capabilities. As a result, we've seen richer media (such as audio and video) become regularly present within the mobile space (see **Figure 4.7**), and consumers are engaging with it.

Figure 4.7 News goes mobile.

This has been especially true within the broadcast genre, including these examples:

1 News channels (see **Figure 4.8**)

2 Entertainment channels

Figure 4.8 Broadcast channel news content.

3 Lifestyle channels

4 Sports channels

5 Weather channels

Mobile Internet

Many broadcast stations have established their own mobile Internet sites. For example, on mobile news channel sites, users can get daily weather reports; read local, national, and global news; and get the latest information on science, health, money, sports, and more. Because news sites use more text than visual design or photographs, they load instantly (even on the slower mobile connections)—thus providing quick access to content. News sites tend to have a much broader target audience. To accommodate their users' various levels of mobile abilities and handsets, news sites follow a "keep it simple" interaction design approach. This approach streamlines content and keeps images minimal, allowing for a seamless click-through experience. Pages are lightweight, and the majority of content on the page is the content itself.

Broadcast channels are also offering up their own media streams on their mobile sites, through mobile applications, or by teaming up with third-party vendors to handle the feeds. This extends broadcast content into the mobile space and allows the regular viewers to stay in touch with channel offerings while on the go. This includes all genres of broadcast channels.

For example, an entertainment broadcast channel might offer up movie previews, full broadcasts, music videos, interviews, or anything else attributed to its programming. Additional support material on entertainment mobile sites can include schedules, show descriptions, cast descriptions, and additional content offerings complementary to the broadcasts themselves. For sports enthusiasts, mobile Internet sites devoted to sports mean they can follow their favorite teams or sports no matter where they are. Fans can follow their teams outside of their living rooms—while riding buses or waiting in lines.

Many broadcast stations have begun to promote their mobile sites on-air, so that viewers are aware of their available mobile content. This has been accomplished via on-air anchor promotions, printing on the screen, and inviting viewers to text short codes to receive corresponding SMSs.

SMS

In addition to creating mobile Internet awareness campaigns, many broadcast programs have been running their own SMS campaigns. Television viewing has truly become interactive, as viewers now have a say or vote on game shows, reality shows, and sportscasts. Some uses of SMS include:

■ **Text the keyword "A, B, C, or D" to 12345 to vote for your favorite contestant or player.** Many times we see reality shows or game shows where a national audience votes on their favorite contestant. The results are tallied via the incoming SMS and displayed in the next day's show. Sportscasts also play in this space, allowing users to vote on the game's MVP. Although this is a small interaction, this is a big step from the days when users only viewed a game show, unable to participate. Now they can participate in the comfort of their living rooms and view the tallied results on television.

■ **Text the keyword "tickets" to 12345 for your chance to win tickets to a game.** Sportscasts give away tickets to upcoming games via SMS. Users submit their SMS: If they win, they receive a confirmation pin and instructions on how to claim their tickets.

■ **Text the keyword "info" to 12345 to learn more about a product.** Commercials end with URLs pointing to online Internet sites and, more recently, SMS calls to action. When users submit their SMSs, they receive SMSs containing a link to the product's mobile Internet site. By clicking that link, users can then learn more about and/or download ringtones, wallpaper, video, and more exclusive mobile content.

- **Text your area code to 12345 to find the weather in your area.** News and weather stations offer a service whereby users SMS their area codes and receive up-to-date weather reports for their areas.

Third-Party Services

Third-party mobile providers have developed applets that stream video 24/7. These applets provide channel viewing of almost every genre, including major broadcast networks and cable networks. Additional streams are also specially produced and unique to the mobile space.

Many third-party vendors have teamed up with core media channels to boost their channel selection and better serve their consumers. These are paid subscription applets, in which users will pay an additional amount per month to run the application. With heavy content such as streaming or downloadable media, users must have an unlimited data plan (or they'll end up with an expensive bill at the end of the month).

With the continual increase in handset and applet development, the presence of broadcast streaming takes another step toward full integration. Network carriers also value the importance of richer media and offer it along with their core services.

Some carriers have invested a great amount of time and development in handset-specific applications that run only on their networks to support such media. See Figure 4.9. These applications stream media directly to users' handsets. This greatly helps out an audience primarily comprised of those new to the mobile Internet. These users might not fully understand how to navigate their way around or how to properly connect to media streams.

Figure 4.9 Device-specific applications.

Radio to Mobile

Radio, which has always been a portable medium, is now successfully integrated with the mobile space. Radio can be listened to in the car, at the gym, in the park—basically anywhere. Mobile can be accessed in many of these same spaces. Integration between the two only makes sense. Some examples of how radio and mobile have integrated are:

■ SMS

■ Concerts

■ Mobile Internet

- Audio streaming
- Ringtones

SMS

SMS plays a big role in radio broadcasts. Communication between radio stations and listeners has always taken place via phone and as a two-way process.

Many stations are now accepting SMS as a form of communication. Listeners can place requests, participate in contests, or subscribe to SMS services set up by the station. If the radio station is a news station, listeners can subscribe to news or traffic alerts. If the station is a sports station, listeners can subscribe to game scores. If the station is music station, listeners can subscribe to free music downloads or concert schedules. The use of SMS adds another opportunity for instant contact between the station and the listener, traditionally achieved only via voice.

Concert Integration

Many radio stations on the entertainment side are responsible for concert promotion and festivals, and mobile has found its way into these areas for promotional purposes. SMS can be utilized to offer free tickets, backstage passes, T-shirts, and other prizes. These contests can be offered both over the air and at the concerts themselves. When the contest takes place at a concert, the execution of the SMS transaction needs to be as simple as possible and timed just right. One example is a scenario in which the first user to respond with the correct answer to a trivia question wins a prize. Common users don't have to think twice about their submissions. The exclusive content must be timely, such as when the center stage of the concert is taking a break or is in transition between sets.

Mobile Internet

Many radio stations have stepped into the mobile Internet space as well, making their playlists available, listing their program schedules, or taking song requests. Radio stations often have a web site as well, which means they are strongly represented in three spaces:

- Radio
- Internet
- Mobile Internet

Much of the content and functionality are interchangeable, but it leverages the portability factors of mobile.

FIGURE 4.10 An example of a podcast.

Podcasts and Audio Streaming via Mobile

One major advantage for radio broadcasts and mobile is audio itself. Many stations are turning to mobile to either stream their broadcasts live or to serve it up as podcasts. These audiocasts can be accessed via a radio station's mobile Internet site, or downloaded from its online Internet site, and synced with their handsets. Users can listen to their favorite sportscasts live (see **FIGURE 4.10**), hear the latest news, or simply enjoy their favorite music. Radio remains portable—as it has from its inception. Mobile helps to enhance this because it brings it into another space. This also means one less device for users to carry.

Ringtones

As a sense of promotion, radio stations sometimes offer ringtones of current songs or jingles. Users can download these from the station's Internet site and sync locally with their handsets; download via the station's mobile site directly to their handsets; or even receive the ringtone via MMS (Multimedia Messaging Service), where the ringtone is sent along with an SMS. This content provides users with an opportunity to "brand" their phones with the station identity or a particular music genre.

Multichannel

A multichannel promotion or campaign has the most impact for brands or projects. This means fully taking advantage of print opportunities, broadcast, web, and mobile opportunities all in one cohesive experience.

The primary goal of a multichannel project is to have the content lead users into another media channel, such as web, print, or broadcast. The content needs to carry over, not replicate itself, where the story continues. For example, if a broadcast commercial is on television, the web portion must not be just the commercial but also interactive content that supports the commercial with stories relevant to the concept. The mobile piece needs to play off that and offer a unique piece of interactivity available only in the mobile space. Print can also point to the mobile execution where users can gain more knowledge about the product and its full story.

Multichannel campaigns must not be forced. Forced campaigns result in dull or replicated content. With users paying mobile and data bills each month, mobile project creators need to be sensitive to what they're serving up and how much of it they're serving. Is the content worth the experience? Is it valuable enough for users who don't typically go into the mobile space to explore the mobile space for the project? Is the mobile channel being used wisely? Most importantly, never use SMS to push spam. Not only will users opt-out of the current project, they'll choose to not participate in future mobile projects.

Multichannel pieces can also work with art gallery exhibits. Such pieces do not always need to be commercial based, focused on brand marketing and awareness. Multichannel simply means awareness and use of other channels to provide an overhaul strategy between different mediums. It keeps viewers engaged with the content and keeps them exploring the project through different means. Print gives users something. Motion video gives users something. Audio gives users something. Mobile gives users something.

Conclusion

Communicating with an audience requires a lot of thought. The message needs to reach the audience in their own space, without any extra search. In addition, the message must be tailored to match both the audience's interaction and communication styles.

An overly experiential message may overwhelm select audiences, while other audiences may fall in love with it. Choosing the proper mode of communication and approach towards a project will allow the communication to transmit properly.

Always aim for a memorable experience—something that provides an element of surprise to intrigue users in each channel. If the payoff for each climactic state is high, users are more likely to continue their journey into the next space. If the experience falls short, then users may simply stop. If the goal of the project is to bring users to the mobile space from print, broadcast, web, or radio channels, those channels need to have a strong enough impact to effectively navigate those users along the path that includes each mode of communication.

5

Designing for Your Audience and Their Handsets

Understanding users' behavior and how they interact within the mobile landscape plays a critical role in the mobile development process. Gathered market intelligence allows development teams to apply their findings to strategic roadmaps and improve a project's execution. Not only does this assist with the presentation of content, but also in the desired delivery method for the target audience. Each method presents new challenges, explorations, and creative opportunities.

Using Statistics

Knowing a project's target audience is the first step into any project. Who is the audience? Is the proposed project idea properly suited for them? Will the audience respond to the project's goals as expected? These questions set the general premises for the project, which require additional statistics to support the target audience behaviors.

Market intelligence, such as mMetrics, provides detailed data reports that include user demographics, carrier information, user engagement information, data plan information, and so on. These reports are a comprehensive analysis of the target audiences' mobile landscape. Direct user behavior is measured on more commonly used channels, while baseline metrics provide valuable insight on key market trends and various areas of interest. This data helps developers determine the proper delivery method for their projects.

For example, if a project is to be generated in Flash Lite, but the statistics return low penetration in this space, the project may also be generated in J2ME to support a larger audience. If a project is a more "general audience" project, such as those found in museums, marketing statistics help determine the most common form of delivery necessary.

The mobile landscape is a constantly changing environment, where the common order of accessibility plays an important factor. When a means of communication is not accessible to the target audience, choose the next closest approach. This order is typically as follows:

1 IVR

2 SMS

3 MMS

4 Mobile sites and general WiFi experiences

5 Bluetooth

6 Applications, such as those created with J2ME

7 Flash Lite and/or any other custom media players that need to be downloaded and installed prior to viewing the experience

A project is never 100 percent compatible across all handsets and audiences, but statistical data allows developers to fine-tune their final products for the core audience.

The User and the Handset

Developing for the mobile environment works much like a puzzle with constantly moving gears. Handsets are continually changing, carriers are continually upgrading their specifications/requirements, and the audience is continually adapting to new interactive interfaces and trends. As each new handset model is released, convergence increases and the cycle continues to evolve.

The audience acts as one piece of this puzzle. How do the users engage with their mobile phones and where do they engage with them? Do they partake in downloads, updates, and mobile applets? Do they have a data plan capable of supporting mobile Internet? At what speed are they consuming media? Is the audience savvy enough to understand the mobile environment and navigate their way through it?

The handset itself acts as another piece of this puzzle. All handset OEMs are different, as well as the carriers in which these operate on. Knowledge of these statistics plays an important role in determining the approach selected for a project. Variants in the manufacturers, carriers, and data plans all impact how a project is delivered. Constant convergence creates a challenging development environment because the variables are constantly changing as well.

Not only does convergence allow for creative growth, but as new handsets are released on the market, users are trained to learn new behavioral methods. In order to stay involved with these evolution cycles, developers focus on four fundamental statistics:

1 **Mobile carriers.** Carriers are frequently changing the way in which they operate. Data plans are changing, allowing users to spend more time accessing mobile Internet content, SMS/MMS, and so on. As users engage more within this space, they learn more about how to navigate the mobile space, they learn new user interfaces, and they also learn the capabilities of their handsets.

2 **Handset OEMs.** As new versions of handsets come out, enhancements are made based on the way users interacted with previous models. As the models get better with each release, users also get better at operating them. It is a progressive path towards handset development.

3 **Platform vendors.** Platform vendors continue to adapt to the new models and new carrier rules/options, allowing for new opportunities in the market. For example, if more handsets and carriers support streaming video, more platform vendors may begin to support this as a service.

4 **Media companies and distribution services.** As handsets support more advanced mobile content and functionality, media companies and advertisers move more into this space, with richer presentations of content. They can also strategically place content in similar mobile spaces to get more traffic. This is similar to the web model in its early stages.

Three additional statistics directly related to users and how they consume mobile content are measured in the following spaces:

1 **Channels.** What content are users navigating to? What content are users viewing on a daily basis? What is the average time per week they are spending in this space?

2 **Devices.** What are the top 25 devices per user/region demographic? Are they on iPhones? Sidekicks? Blackberries? Nine-button handsets? Do we see users upgrading one device for another? What three applications or functions are they using most on these devices?

3 **Content offerings.** Are users taking advantage of content that is readily available to them? Do users know where to find mobile content specific to their liking? Are they engaging with factory-installed handset applications? Are users receptive to purchasing additional data plans, applications, and third-party services to receive additional content? Do they know what's out there?

Without this knowledge, very little success can be achieved.

Development

The three main targets of mobile development are:

1 Compatibility

2 Flexibility

3 Size

Compatibility

Compatibility can be achieved with proper handset detection. This detection can be applied to any execution, whether it be SMS based, third-party installation based, or a mobile Internet experience. If detection is set up successfully, the proper corresponding build components are served up to the user.

Flexibility

Flexibility comes from a dynamic file structure. As seen in other environments, a dynamic file architecture allows for extensive growth over time and ease of updates. A shared resource repository with an online desktop experience is even more beneficial, which means the same data powering an online experience may also power the mobile experience. This technique keeps both channels current and fresh.

Centralized data is a key component to any project. The ability to share data amongst mediums allows one single change to the core to reflect on the receiving components. For example, if an online desktop experience exists, a mobile project can be configured to share the same data sets that power the .com experience. Whether it's a mobile web project, downloadable applet, or other experience, the ability to share data/assets enables a very smart developer build. If the project is a downloadable application, such as a J2ME or Flash Lite piece, a remote connection allows the application to pull its data from a remote server.

Size

Maintaining a manageable file size is key for a successful mobile experience. The goal is to achieve the smallest possible file sizes, so that the interaction between the user and technology is seamless. Larger files mean longer download times. Because carrier speeds vary greatly, from very slow to WiFi, both the code and the image size need to be factored into the overall size of a page load or download.

If the mobile project is an application, some handsets have very limited file space—under 2 MB total. If users already have cellphone pics and other personal content stored on their handsets, the application may have trouble installing. Some handsets with smaller memory space even have trouble displaying mobile sites when the memory is close to filled. This is especially true when viewing media files, such as audio and video.

Serving Up Options

Always keep in mind the alternative experience when developing. This allows the project to reach a broader group within the target audience. No build will reach everyone. There are too many factors involved, even with porting.

The best is to aim for the highest common denominator in that group and provide alternative experiences for those that might not be in the higher percentage. For example, an application may reach only those capable of having handsets supporting the application. However, the same content could reach a larger audience if it were a mobile site.

With mobile Internet sites, a smart architecture utilizes the same set of core build files, with alternative CSS documents. The proper CSS is served up via the incoming handset detection results and is hooked into the corresponding front-end templates. The front-end templates can be built in PHP, WML, AJAX, JHTML, and so on. The idea of the centralized code base allows for a more robust build capable of accommodating growth as time goes by. With the rapid growth in the marketplace, updates need to take place only in one location to support handset changes. Having too many files causes more of a tedious task when updating arises. Code transcendence allows one update to carry through the multiple frameworks at `state`.

When working with Java and Flash Lite applets, they typically look for the `screen.width` and `screen.height` to determine the proper sizing and scale accordingly. The initial visual design for these executions should accommodate this spacing, as well as the internal font sizing. Readability is an important factor in these applications, since many times these are more financial- or location-based applications, where the main focus is information.

Developing with Java requires knowledge of CLDC (Connected Limited Device Configuration) and MIDP (Mobile Information Device Profile). Java applications are typically ported across handsets based on these specs and handset sizes. The CLDC is a fundamental part of the architecture of the Java 2 Platform,

Micro Edition (J2ME). J2ME technology is delivered in API bundles called configurations, profiles, and optional packages. A J2ME application environment includes both a configuration like CLDC and a profile like the MIDP. Additional Java packages provide capability specific to an area of functionality. Examples include multimedia capabilities, media playback, and wireless messaging.

Flash Lite development uses the ActionScript language. ActionScript is the language also used in the Adobe Flash desktop experience. Many Flash developers explore Flash Lite at some point in their studies. Flash Lite is an interesting approach towards interactivity on the handset. Capable of supporting animations and various multimedia components, it gives visual designers a bit more control on how the interactivity should work. Flash Lite requires users to have the Flash Lite player on their handsets. At the time of this book's printing, these numbers are still relatively low, thus making this a lower penetration for any target audience.

Smart phone development is another form of this more concentrated focus. These builds are specific to their native platforms—PALM, Windows, and/or Apple. Each version of the platform may require its own unique build depending on what attributes are included in the programming. Since these applications are specific to these platforms, alternative apps are typically served up in order to reach a broader audience. Solely developing for a smart phone can prove an expensive bill if porting to other traditional handsets is required. The costs add up quite quickly.

Porting

Porting is the process of taking a preexisting mobile build and migrating it across different handsets and/or development environments. For example, a J2ME mobile game may need to be modified to work across various handsets within the target audience. Modifications are implemented so that the applet will run flawlessly on the other devices, especially when there are different versions of Java running on each handset.

While some handsets do share some core manufacturer similarities, many handsets still vary enough that an additional modification is necessary for that build to deploy properly. Typically one core build will be developed for the primary handset of the target audience and based on gathered market intelligence of the top 25 handsets (the build then gets modified for each).

In addition, porting can refer to rewriting a mobile build into another format for mobile. When a project is ported into another format, not only does the programming environment change but the content presentation is also re-examined to assure a smart experience. Each channel and execution is unique. Content should always remain the focus of the porting process—the interactivity should carry through fluently. Technology is merely the delivery of the message.

Handset Detection

Once the programming build has been completed, handset detection is implemented to assure that the users have been delivered the proper format for their devices. Handset detection can assist in serving up the properly formatted ringtone, mobile Internet page, mobile video, Java applet, and so on. With over 5,000 handsets on the market, handset detection's main task is to properly read the incoming device and properly map it with the corresponding content. For those devices that may not be mapped properly, an alternative default experience may be served. No build is 100 percent compatible across all handsets.

Handset detection is built into the http request using programming schemata such as WURFL. WURFL (Wireless Universal Resource File) is an open source XML configuration file that contains a repository of well over 5,000 global devices. The goal

A complete list of WURFL capabilities, along with their descriptions, is located at http://wurfl.sourceforge.net/help_doc.php.

of the WURFL project is to document all of the capabilities present in global devices. WURFL works while providing a simple API to programmatically query the repository and serve up the appropriate formatted content.

The device detection returns the device's values, and the correct content or CSS is served up. WURFL is a cost-effective method for handset detection, while other options on the market are paid services. WURFL is the common choice of handset detection for most programmers. See **FIGURE 5.1**.

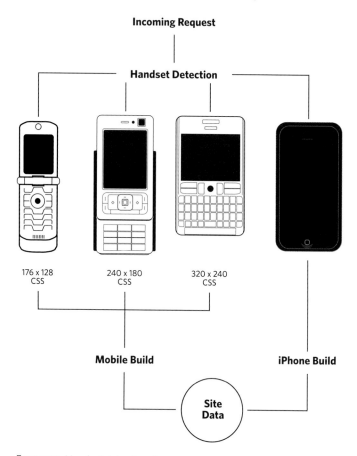

FIGURE 5.1 Handset detection flow.

The WURFL XML structure is similar to the following:

```
<wurfl>
  <devices>
    <device ...>
      <group ...>
        <capability name="..." value="...">
          :
      </group>
        :
    </device>
      :
  </devices>
</wurfl>
```

A fragment example of data returned in this structure looks similar to the following, depending on the specifics of the developer's query:

```
<device user_agent="Nokia3100" actual_device_
root="true"
        fall_back="nokia_generic_series40"
        id="nokia_3100_ver1">
  <group id="product_info">
    <capability name="model_name" value="3100"/>
  </group>
  <group id="xhtml_ui">
    <capability name="xhtml_format_as_css_property"
value="true"/>
    <capability name="xhtml_supports_table_for_
layout" value="true"/>
    <capability name="xhtml_supports_css_cell_table_
coloring" value="true"/>
    <capability name="xhtml_readable_background_
color1" value="#99CCFF"/>
```

```
    <capability name="xhtml_readable_background_
color2" value="#FFFFFF"/>

  </group>

  <group id="markup">

    <capability name="preferred_markup" value="html_
wi_oma_xhtmlmp_1_0"/>

    <capability name="html_wi_w3_xhtmlbasic"
value="true"/>

    <capability name="html_wi_oma_xhtmlmp_1_0"
value="true"/>

  </group>

</device>
```

The `<device>` element represents the incoming device and contains all the specific features of that device. This includes:

- `User Agent String`

- `Device ID`

- `Fall_back` attribute, which gives a way to infer more information regarding the device. This is typically the device ID
  of another handset.

Handset Testing

Handset testing is crucial to any form of mobile development.
This testing takes place during the entire development phase,
with a more detail-oriented form before deployment. There are
three ways handset testing can and should be accomplished:

- User agents and desktop emulators (development phase)

- Virtual emulators (final phase development)

- Real handsets (QA phase)

User agents and desktop emulators are available as browser
plug-ins for Firefox, Safari, Opera, and Internet Explorer.
These emulators, while not as ideal as testing on a virtual
or real handset, do provide a safe development environment

for developmental testing. These emulators can simulate the behaviors of the actual devices with relative similarities, but they cannot simulate the carrier-specific variables associated with mobile networks. For more Java-based applets, an emulator is typically packaged with the J2ME programming environment. This allows the developer to simulate a true runtime environment before testing on the handsets themselves.

Testing on actual handsets is the most assured way of achieving mobile success. Emulators provide a relatively strong base reference, but variables in carrier traits and differences in carriers cause inconsistent results in testing.

 A series of user agent and desktop emulators can be downloaded from the following locations:

- Opera Software AG (www.opera.com)
- Firefox User Agent Switcher (http://chrispederick.com/work/useragentswitcher/)
- Firefox Web Developers Toolbar (http://chrispederick.com/work/webdeveloper)
- Firebug (www.getfirebug.com)
- dotMobi Online Phone Emulator (http://emulator.mtld.mobi/)
- Nokia Browser Simulator (www.forum.nokia.com/info/sw.nokia.com/id/db2c69a2-4066-46ff-81c4-caac8872a7c5/NMB40_install.zip.html)
- Openwave Phone Simulator (http://developer.openwave.com/dvl/member/downloadManager.htm?softwareId=23)
- Opera Mini Simulator (www.opera.com/products/mobile/operamini/demo.dml)

Virtual emulators are those online services where users can preview their builds on a real handset via Internet connection. These sites allow users to connect to handsets stored in a lab location and bring their interfaces up within the web browser for viewing. DeviceAnywhere (www.deviceanywhere.com/) is an example of this. Developers can post their builds on a web server and bring the URL up in the virtual device.

The most accurate and final form of handset testing is on real devices. Typically the project is tested on the top 25 handsets of the target audience, each device providing a range of screen sizes, carriers, and media support. This approach provides the most absolute form of feedback for any build and determines what areas need to be adjusted visually and functionally.

Handset testing requires dedication and concentration. Each handset and its browser will always offer different results. For example, two similar manufacturer devices may offer completely different results when operating on different networks. The most effective way to test is on the actual handsets, by running on variable networks. This QA process is a much more cumbersome, detail-oriented process than that of a typical desktop experience. Patience is a virtue.

Quality Assurance

As previously discussed in this chapter, some carriers may prevent application downloads/installations and/or restrict certain media playbacks, such as streaming video. Some of the target audience's top 25 handsets may also be missing key software components, such as those necessary for specific media formats, applications, or audio formats. Hard drive space also plays a key factor when dealing with larger media, such as audio and video. Users must have enough drive space to save the mobile product and enough space left for optimal performance.

When performing quality assurance tests, each approach has its own set of challenges to examine. The following examples are the backbone for each channel. Once these areas pass QA tests, details specific to that project must be examined and thoroughly tested.

SMS

Carrier approval for new SMS campaigns can take anywhere from four to six weeks to approve, depending on details.

- Secure and purchase vanity short code (approximately $12,000/year)
- Achieve carrier approval for campaign
- 160 maximum character limit on outgoing SMS
- All active links display as clickable links within outgoing SMS

Ringtone

Carrier approval for new MMS campaigns can take anywhere from six to eight weeks to approve, depending on details.

- Campaign carrier approval
- Handset detection
- MMS file formats for select models (WAV, MP3, WMV, and so on)
- MMS file size vs. available device disk space
- Proper AAC encoding
- Properly looped files
- Proper naming convention recognizable for the handsets
- Proper MMS deployment or http download

Video

All video tests should be performed using a sample video representative of the project's video compression settings. This sample video should pass through all the following tests before compressing out the project's additional videos:

- Handset detection
- Proper video compression
- Proper streaming rate *(when applicable)*
- Proper streaming server configuration *(when applicable)*

- File size vs. available device storage space
- Handset processor vs. video bit rate
- Compatible with handset media players
- Compatible with carriers that allow for streaming
- Compatible with carriers that allow for http downloads

Applets

Applet testing is a time-consuming process. If an applet fails, it will need to be revisited, reprogrammed, reinstalled, and retested. This process is "repeat as necessary" for each individual handset that the applet lives on. The following list demonstrates the core areas of testing, in addition to the applet's project specifics:

- Handset detection
- Top 25 ported versions of the application
- Ease of applet installation
- Required applet storage space
- Applet specifics vs. device manufacturer capabilities
- Local data storage vs. remote data storage
- Content scalability
- Image clarity
- Text clarity
- Audio performance
- Video performance
- Compatible with carriers that allow for http downloads

Mobile Site

Mobile sites should be tested on the top 25 target audience handsets across the various carrier networks that these handsets may reside on. This ensures you've tested all possible scenarios between manufacturers and carriers. The core fundamentals to look for, in addition to the project's specifics, are:

- Handset detection

- Load time

- Content scalability

- Image clarity

- Text clarity

- Audio performance per above specifications

- Video performance per above specifications

- Compatible with carriers that allow for http downloads

Bluetooth

Bluetooth projects are typically created for use in a public space, so a series of items and obstacles need to be addressed to ensure a safe data transfer between the broadcasting device and the user handset.

- Legal approvals associated with broadcasting in certain vicinities

- Placement of broadcaster vs. audience position

- Base signal strength

- Environmental conditions vs. signal strength

- Ease of interactivity

- Permission

- Delivery of content

IVR

IVR testing requires additional coordination with the IVR vendor or operators to assure all logic and bandwidth is properly set up for the project. Items such as the following are often tested alongside the project specifics:

- Secured call-in number

- Waiting room support

- Participant bandwidth

- Playback scenarios
- Connection scenarios
- External components

Overall Concept

The technical phase is one aspect of quality assurance testing; the other aspect is the project itself. The project needs to make itself worthy of deployment, and this can be realistically examined when the build is on the handset and is in testers' hands.

- Is the payoff worth the mobile execution?
- What is asked of the audience in order to participate?
- How many steps are involved in the whole process? If more than one or two, rethink.
- Is it too difficult for them to grasp?
- Does the piece involve SMS spam—no!
- Are any specific media players/plug-ins required for installation prior to viewing?

Conclusion

With the ever-increasing demand for new, enhanced mobile features and the release of new handsets on the market each week, there is never a 100 percent flawless project out there. The goal with mobile development is to aim for both your target audience and the highest common denominator of mass audience devices. Always provide an alternative solution, no matter how small it may be. Simple navigation systems along with a simple site design can still present a compelling experience if the content is compelling. If the content is not compelling, the experience should not even exist.

6

Interaction Design

As digital media like the web and mobile become more perva-sive in our everyday lives, the role of interaction design becomes crucial to the success of a mobile experience. Designing for two-way interactive media cannot be looked upon the same way as designing an inanimate object or product. As designers, we must create powerful experiences that fit into people's everyday lives. It is not just about how the experience visually looks, but how it behaves—every screen, every click, every bit of information displayed determines the quality of the user experience.

When designing for mobile, we must place serious consideration toward where the software will be used, what it will be used for, and what the target mobile operating system and mobile device will be. Will the mobile site or application be designed for an iPhone environment, a Google Android environment, or a Symbian environment?

In this chapter, we will first discuss the role that interaction design plays in creating useful mobile sites and applications. We'll also talk about the special implications to consider when designing for the small screen. Given the limited screen real estate and unique input techniques of mobile devices, an even greater emphasis should be placed upon the interaction design phase of a mobile project. Next, we'll review the proper inter-action design process and the various methods used in cre-ating interaction design deliverables. Some of those methods include target device analysis, user research, persona creation, sketching, and interaction design schematics. We'll close out the chapter by leaving you with enough information resources to go off and begin your own work.

Designing for the Small Screen

"Trying to type on mobile is like trying to remove a contact lens with a cotton ball — it's just not fun." [1]

—*Aza Raski*

---

1   www.smallsurfaces.com/2008/06/firefox-mobile-concept-video/ Aza Raski

Designing for small screens has always been one of the biggest challenges for the mobile medium. When compared with the PC, smaller screen sizes have always challenged designers to come up with innovative solutions to maximize screen real estate.

Mobile devices have evolved into powerful convergent devices with better processor capabilities, sharper screen resolution, better color display, and better overall features. The technology has evolved to a point where powerful mobile applications and mobile sites can now be used on the mobile phone. However, the devices still remain small when compared to PCs, and migrating full-size PC applications and/or web sites to the mobile device remains a bad idea. Not all design concepts that work in a PC environment can be successful on mobile devices.

Additionally, if we look out into the landscape of mobile devices, we see a landscape littered with thousands of mobile devices with different capabilities, and different screen size resolutions.

In Barbara Ballard's book *Designing the Mobile User Experience*, she talks of mobilizing, not miniaturizing, full-size, PC-based web sites and/or applications. Mobile sites or applications need to be optimized for the mobile experience. Expecting to completely transfer an existing web site or PC application to the mobile device is a recipe for a poor user experience. This section covers some reasons why designers need to mobilize, not miniaturize, PC-based experiences for mobile.

Varying Input Modalities

Most devices are standard clamshell or flip phones with access to a standard phone keypad, a left soft key, a right soft key, and a four-way directional keypad with a center select button. See FIGURE 6.1.

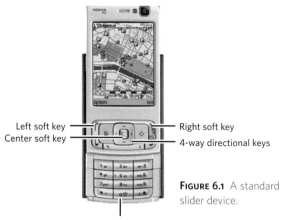

Left soft key
Center soft key
Right soft key
4-way directional keys

FIGURE 6.1 A standard slider device.

Standard mobile phone keypad

Other devices like the Apple iPhone are leading the next gen-eration of multi-touch-screen mobile devices. These devices lack the standard input modalities that users have grown accustomed to. They also lack any form of soft keys or four-way directional keys. A good majority of a user's input is via a touch interface. See **FIGURE 6.2**.

FIGURE 6.2 An iPhone multi-touch.

Unless you optimize an existing web site or application for mobile, your designs will more than likely not support various input modalities via mobile devices. Imagine using a four-way directional keypad on your mobile phone to navigate a web site with over 100 live links. Users would have to click 100 times to get to the last link. Additionally, PC-based web sites often serve up standard hyperlinks that are difficult to click with a fingertip when using a touch-screen device. Mobile sites for Digg.com, Facebook, and ESPN optimize their interfaces to accommodate a touch-based input modality.

Varying Screen Sizes

Interaction design optimized to support varying screen sizes is mandatory these days. If you believe in the mantra that your user experience is your brand and your brand is your user experience, then perfect mobile page rendering is a must. Designs that are not optimized for varying screen sizes can create situations where some designs: **a.** don't utilize the full screen real estate, **b.** are off center, or **c.** bleed off the page and require an unnatural left-to-right scrolling.

The folks over at the Sender11 blog did a great study about mobile screen size trends, and their findings reveal that over the years screen size has definitely increased. Most of the larger screens have gone with a landscape orientation, while smaller devices typically stick to a portrait orientation. The study also noted that some of the newer devices on the market can change orientation so they work both in landscape and portrait. Overall, 240 x 320 (QVGA) is the dominant screen size in the market, and that particular size specification is rapidly being adopted by most handset manufacturers.

When optimizing design for varying screen size, the screen width is really the main thing to worry about. Page height can easily be accommodated by vertical scrolling. However, no one enjoys a horizontal scroll experience. Also keep in mind that 240 x 320 is the dominant screen size, but don't forget to design for the 176px-wide device. There are still enough 176px-wide devices in the market to design for, albeit most handset manufacturers seem to be decommissioning 176px-wide and 128px-wide devices.[2] See **FIGURE 6.3**.

 www.usshortcodes.com/csc_best_practices.html

---

2   http://sender11.typepad.com/sender11/2008/04/mobile-screen-s.html

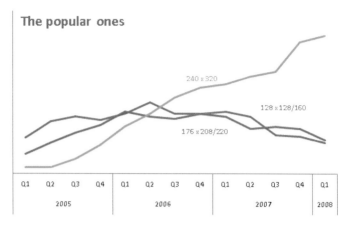

The popular ones

240 x 320

128 x 128/160

176 x 208/Z20

| Q1 | Q2 | Q3 | Q4 | Q1 | Q2 | Q3 | Q4 | Q1 | Q2 | Q3 | Q4 | Q1 |
| 2005 | | | | 2006 | | | | 2007 | | | | 2008 |

Figure 6.3 240px-wide (QVGA) devices are growing in popularity.[3]

A couple of key tidbits to keep in mind when designing for smaller mobile screen sizes:

■ Create simple, organized page designs that limit any form of horizontal scrolling. Don't be afraid of using tabs, pull-downs, and multiple pages to keep your page designs clean and simple.

■ Provide an easy way for users to return to the home page, access the main menu, and navigate back one level. Breadcrumbs allow users to track themselves within the mobile experience. "Tuck away" the main menu and allow users to utilize the soft keys to quickly access it.

■ Make the screen size feel bigger than it actually is. If necessary, utilize techniques like zooming in and out, panning, and page leafing to create the illusion of larger screen sizes.

Varying Capabilities

Although mobile devices are evolving and becoming more powerful, a good majority of mobile browsers still cannot support Flash animations or stream QuickTime movies or podcasts directly in the browser environment. As a result, one critical step involved in mobilizing web content is to strip away content that

3 http://sender11.typepad.com/sender11/2008/04/mobile-screen-s.html

cannot be rendered on certain mobile devices. No one wants to see broken links or empty content blocks on a mobile site where a Flash movie was supposed to play.

On the flip side of stripping away content, designers and developers should create interactions that leverage the varying capabilities of mobile browsers. Some mobile browsers can even support special features like "page sliding." The current Digg.com iPhone site does a good job at using this "page sliding" feature. FIGURE 6.4 shows a comparison of a mobile optimized site for Digg.com versus what the full Web site would look like rendered on the iPhone.

FIGURE 6.4
An Apple iPhone-optimized version of Digg.com compared to a full version of Digg.com rendered in the iPhone browser.

Varying User Expectations

We live in a world where there is so much content available but users have little time to navigate through the mounds and mounds of it. Users are increasingly consuming their content in small doses. As a result, the continuing trend for mobile content developers is to provide bite-size experiences to align with users' expectations of the medium. Most users don't want to watch a feature-length movie on their mobile devices, nor do they want every single possible article republished from NYTimes.com. The TV, PC, and print mediums will be the destination spots for long-form and richer content experiences.

Mobile users are typically on the go or just finding a few free minutes in the day to "snack" on content. Mobile is the perfect medium for "snackable" content. The content can be delivered in two or three lines of text, an abbreviated mobile site, or in a short 30-second video or audio clip. As a result, designers should create content experiences that leverage this expectation and behavior. Even with new devices that support bigger screens and faster network speeds, just moving all TV, PC, and print content over to mobile without restrategizing and/or redesigning is a recipe for bad user experience.

Varying User Behavior

The true differentiator of mobile is dynamic content based on time, location, and social awareness. This does not apply to other mediums like TV, web, or print. Mobile designers should focus on this difference and its implications because users' behavior while mobile is different than users' behavior when tethered to their PCs. When users shift from place to place, their content should change based on time, location, and social awareness.

Leveraging Built-In Hardware and Features on a Mobile Phone

Mobile applications can leverage built-in hardware on a mobile phone like integrated GPS chips, built-in cameras, and video recorders. Mobile applications can also access users' contact lists and scan through their media files to add further depth and personalization to the user experience.

One great example of a mobile application that taps into a mobile device's built-in hardware is the Nokia Sports Tracker. See **FIGURE 6.5**. The Nokia Sports Tracker mobile application utilizes the built-in GPS hardware on a mobile device to track the speed, distance, and time for users during sporting activities.

This is a good example of how leveraging built-in hardware essentially makes the application worthwhile and possible. If designers simply "miniaturized" existing web applications, then they would miss out on fully leveraging these new mobile capabilities.

FIGURE 6.5 The Nokia SportsTracker application leverages a built-in GPS chip.

What Is the Mobile Interaction Design Process?

Interaction design helps create a user experience based on user requirements. It lays down a framework for how a mobile site or application is organized, how it's presented to users, and how those users navigate or interact with the site or application. It also deals with different "states" of the experience and system feedback to the user.

Interaction design schematics will serve as a specification document for visual designers and programmers. It will also allow them to further work on bringing your mobile site or application to life.

In a perfect world, the interaction design process will involve user research to better understand the needs of the users first-hand. User research will then provide enough insights to inform a team of interaction designers to begin developing designs that can be prototyped and tested (multiple times if necessary) to determine whether or not the overall user experience is usable and optimally designed.

Much of what we will cover in the next few sections will mirror the interaction design process for web-based applications or sites, with some special considerations made for designing for the mobile medium. Essentially, it will be a quick overview of the interaction design process for mobile. If you want to dive deeper into interaction design for mobile, we suggest that you pick up the following two books: *Mobile Interaction Design* by Matt Jones and Gary Marsden and *Designing the Mobile User Experience* by Barbara Ballard. Both books drill down to a level of thinking around interaction design that we will only skim over in this book.

The Three Stages of the Mobile Interaction Design Process

We've broken down the mobile interaction design process into the following three stages:

1 User research: understanding the users.

2 Developing designs: bringing ideas to life.

3 Test, learn, and refine: perfecting your ideas.

Figure 6.6 shows the three stages and what is involved with each stage.

+Target Device Analysis
+Ethnographic Studies & User Interviews
+Requirements Gathering

Stage 1: **USER RESEARCH**
Understanding the Users

+Concepting
+Organization
+Interaction Design
+Rapid Prototyping

Stage 2: **DEVELOPING DESIGNS**
Bringing Ideas to Life

+Focus Group Testing
+Usability Testing

Stage 3: **TEST, LEARN, REFINE**
Perfecting Your Ideas

Figure 6.6 The three-stage mobile interaction design process.

Ideally, every interaction designer would have enough time, resources, and budget to step through all three stages of the interaction design process in their entirety. Each stage has a different end goal, and interaction designers will employ various methods to reach these end goals. As we all know, not every project is managed in these "perfect world" conditions, so some stages may be "skimped" on.

STAGE 1: USER RESEARCH

Understand your users and define who they are. Watch what they do in their day-to-day lives. Ask them what they use their mobile devices for. Gain a sense of what mobile devices your target audience is using. As interaction designers, we want to provide users with useful and usable mobile experiences that are grounded in sound user research and strategic design thinking. Once user research is performed, target personas are created based on the user research, and then user goals are identified for each persona.

By the end of this stage, an interaction designer should have completed these three main deliverables:

1 Target device analysis and recommendations.

2 User personas and user goals.

3 User requirements document.

The following section includes a description of each of these deliverables and the associated methods used to create them.

Target Device Analysis and Recommendation

This deliverable is unique to mobile. With the tremendous proliferation of devices in the marketplace, it is almost impossible to create a mobile experience that works on every device. As a result, it is important to identify what target devices your users will have. Once the target devices are identified, a thorough analysis of each device's capabilities should be performed, as well as a recommendation for how design and development should move forward when building out the mobile site or application.

Device fragmentation is a reality of the mobile industry, where multiple standards exist for multiple devices with different browsers, features, and carrier restrictions. My general rule of thumb is to "never" promise a client that a mobile site or application will work on every device in the marketplace.

A better approach is to make one of the following recommendations:

- **Target specific devices.** Identify a limited range of devices that are currently being used heavily by your target audience and design, optimize, and test only for that range of devices. Blackberry applications like the E*Trade Mobile Pro and the Digg.com Apple iPhone Web app are good examples of mobile applications or sites that were created to satisfy a limited range of devices. This approach sets the expectations from a consumer standpoint as to what devices will be supported and allows the design and development teams to focus their time and attention on just a few devices.

- **Dynamic mobile content formatting.** Utilize handset detection that cross-references the WURFL device database, an open source XML configuration file that contains information about device capabilities and features. Once a device's capabilities and features are discovered, you can determine the optimal design specs (CSS) to apply to a core set of XML data. The optimal CSS will then be applied to the XML to present content formatted per the device accessing the content. **Figure 6.7** shows dynamic content formatting.

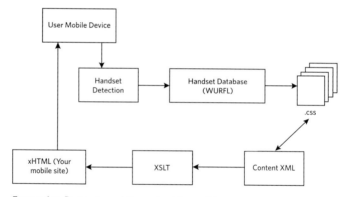

Figure 6.7 Dynamic mobile content formatting.

Since the WURFL device database is open source and constantly in flux as new devices come to market, you should design and develop your mobile site or application to degrade gracefully to account for missing or erroneous device information in WURFL.

User Personas and User Goals

User personas are representations of the different user types within your target audience. User personas are the foundation of any user-centered design process for designing any digital experience. The intention of creating user personae is for designers to better uncover users' goals and needs when designing a mobile site or application. User personas will serve as the foundation for guiding decisions when it comes to determining features and design decisions around your mobile site or application. Ideally, personas are created based on information garnered during ethnographic studies and user interviews. Ethnographic studies and user interviews are the two main methods for creating user personae and user goals.

Personas are typically descriptions that highlight user behaviors, user goals, and attitudes toward technology and media. **Figure 6.8** shows a sample persona. Personas help interaction designers work toward designing for real users and avoid the common pitfall of designing for oneself. Essentially, personas should always be used by designers and developers as a reality check to keep the focus of the work on the common goals of real users.

AMY STARKS
Age 25, DJ / Pilates Instructor
New York, NY

"I want to find what I'm looking for as quickly and easily as possible."

PERSONAL BACKGROUND
Amy is a casual shopper. She is a single, college graduate and in her first job. She did not participate in college or high school sports, but she has always led a fairly active life and is now teaching pilates. She'd like to look good doing it. She's always been drawn to certain brands, but she is on a budget so she will compromise on brand loyalty to save some money. Would love to be alerted about all sales as soon as they happen.

PROFILE
workout time per week: 4-6 hours
top activities: yoga, pilates, walking, swimming, tennis
running importance: low to medium
motivation for playing: personal health, looking good
when does she wear gear: mainly working out
average annual spend: $700
favorite sports gear websites   JC Penny, Amazon
favorite physical stores   Mostly in the mall

SPORTS PARTICIPATION
- "I feel so much better and healthier when I work out. I try to go 4 days a week for 2 hours. I spend my weekends walking around."
- Likes to look attractive at the gym - buys entire outfits for style.

ONLINE ACTIVITY
- "My friends tease me about how much time I spend online. I read the news and look at tips.
- "Shops and explores online often - buys everything she can online.

SHOPPING BEHAVIOR AND PREFERENCES
- Footwear - loves colorful shoes with lots of ankle support.
- Clothing - you have to have dozens of outfits in trendy colors and styles.
- You have to look good at the gym or even walking around on Saturday in track pants.

Figure 6.8 Sample user persona

User Requirements Document

The last deliverable of this stage involves requirements gathering that will lead to the production of a user requirements document. The user requirements document specifies what the users will expect from the mobile site or application. The biggest difficulty is determining what the user actually wants; most users can't clearly communicate their needs and wants. Additionally, most users often provide inaccurate information, so the role of the interaction designer in determining accurate user requirements is a tough task. Interaction designers have to juggle conflicting requirements from various users and stakeholders and ultimately produce a user requirements document.

STAGE 2: DEVELOPING DESIGNS

Based on insights and requirements acquired during the user research stage, this stage is about creating concepts and interaction design schematics that represent the mobile site or application taxonomy, navigation, and functionality. Once these designs are completed, designers should create prototypes that allow for functional demos. These demos will then be used to promote discussions amongst the design team. Improvements to the prototypes can be iterative during this stage. Functional prototypes will then be utilized for formal testing during the next stage: Test, learn, and refine.

By the end of this stage, an interaction designer should have completed these five main deliverables:

1 Concept

2 Sitemap and navigation

3 Rapid paper prototyping or sketching

4 Interaction design schematics

5 Functional prototype

The following section includes a description of each deliverable and the associated methods used to create them.

Concept

This is the first deliverable of stage 2 and before any formal design work can begin, a concept (for example, "The Big Idea" or "The Elevator Pitch") needs to be defined. The concept is an overview description for the mobile site or application. The concept should be succinct: capable of being communicated in one short paragraph or in less than 30 seconds. TechCrunch.com has a great site with a compilation of elevator pitches (in video format) from aspiring startups. Check out the site for examples: http://pitches.techcrunch.com/.

Sitemap and Navigation

Typically when a mobile site or application is more than two levels deep, with many subsections on each level, a sitemap is necessary to define the architecture of the experience. The sitemap provides a general view of the overall contents within your mobile site or application. Creating a sitemap also forces you to create a taxonomy for your content that will essentially lead into how your mobile site or application's navigation structures and menus are organized.

Some interaction designers will utilize the popular card-sorting technique to help drive the creation of a sitemap and logical taxonomy for the content. The simple process of card-sorting (see **FIGURE 6.9**) involves sorting a set of cards (that are labeled with a piece of content or functionality) into groups. These user-generated groups then become the logical mental groupings of content and features that users have. Potentially, each grouping could be a different section within your mobile site or application.

FIGURE 6.9 Card sorting in action.

Rapid Paper Prototyping or Sketching

"Prototype early and often, making each iterative step a little more realistic. At some point you are likely to experience that wonderful "Aha" feeling that comes with a creative leap, but that is only an indication that you have moved forward in the detail of the aspect of the design that you are focusing on right then. You will only know that the design is good when you have tried it out with the people who will use it and found they they are pleased, excited, motivated, and satisfied with the result."

—Bill Moggridge, *Designing Interactions*

One technique used to bring designs to life is rapid paper prototyping. Rapid paper prototyping as a design technique has gained in popularity for developing web applications and could be used equally as a design technique for designing mobile sites or applications. The benefits that rapid paper prototyping provides to the design process are increased collaboration with users, stakeholders, and technologists to create more effective solutions. Paper prototypes allow designers to "work through" design decisions before they move down the long, arduous path of creating interaction design schematics. It is also a technique that allows designers to focus on a design solution and not the documentation before important design choices are made.

Sketching (see **FIGURE 6.10**) is another technique that shares benefits similar to rapid paper prototyping, such as enhanced collaboration with project team members and the ability to help designers "work through" design decisions.

FIGURE 6.10 A sample mobile sketch.

Interaction Design Schematics

This deliverable involves wire-framing the overall mobile site or application experience. As opposed to rapid paper prototyping and sketching, interaction design schematics essentially are deeper dives into how the exact interaction and user flows of a mobile site or application are laid out. Schematics are used to take complex user flows and interactions and make them easy for visual designers and programmers to understand.

Detailed interaction design schematics often serve as documentation for developers and designers to work from. In some cases, schematics can be used to explain to stakeholders how the various pages of a mobile site or application will look and function.

However, in much the same way that interaction design schematics are "evolving" for designing web applications, mobile site or application designers may need to supplement interaction design schematics with functioning prototypes.

As mobile sites or applications begin to support technologies like AJAX, Flash Lite, Silverlight, and Cocoa, we begin to leave the world of page-based interactions. Interaction design schematics begin to fall short in showcasing different possible states of a page. As a result, we will begin to see more importance placed on the functional prototype.

Functional Prototypes

This deliverable typically comes after a design team has spent enough time putting together and thinking through interaction design schematics. Functional prototypes help convey the power of a mobile site or application. Instead of presenting static interaction design schematics or visual designs to a client, a functional prototype can help showcase branded interfaces that show motion and leverage iconic interactions. It also helps the sell-through process with key decision makers. Static interaction design schematics often don't provide the same level of emotional impact as a functional prototype.

Functional prototypes are also great tools to use for focus group testing or usability testing. Compared to static interaction design schematics or visual design boards, putting "live" functional prototypes in front of users is a more effective way of testing usability or validating concepts.

STAGE 3: TEST, LEARN, AND REFINE

This stage is all about putting your designs and prototypes to the test. Testing your designs is important so that you don't waste money executing ideas that don't make sense or are unusable. Whether it's focus-group testing or usability testing, this stage is used to identify strengths and weaknesses of a concept or enable an interaction design team to improve upon its designs. In some cases, it can force a team to start over from scratch.

By the end of this stage, an interaction designer should have completed these two main deliverables:

1 Focus group testing

2 Usability testing

The following sections describe each deliverable and the associated methods used to create them.

Focus Group Testing

Focus group testing typically validates your ideas, concepts, and prototypes by asking a group of qualified and screened people about their attitudes toward your mobile site or application concept and designs. Participants are screened to verify they are part of your target audience. The groups typically consist of 8 to 10 participants; a third-party moderator will often lead the conversation to help probe users' attitudes toward your mobile site or application. A professionally trained moderator can lead the conversation without influencing too much of what the users will say. Moderators will often follow a moderator guide created in conjunction with the design agency that sets the goals for the testing sessions.

Feedback from the group-testing sessions is often collected in a qualitative manner. The strength of focus group testing lies in its ability to allow companies to discuss freely with participants potential concept ideas, design ideas, and design layouts.

Clients, interaction designers, and researchers will often observe the testing sessions behind a one-way mirror. The sessions are often video recorded and transcripts created based on the video recordings. The feedback captured is an invaluable future indicator of whether or not the market will like or dislike the mobile site or application.

Usability Testing

Usability testing evaluates whether your mobile site or application meets its intended purpose. Testing your designs and prototype on real users allows designers to better understand from a usability standpoint what is working, what isn't working, and what can be improved.

Usability testing sessions often take place in one-on-one sessions, where users are observed using your mobile site or application. Prior to the testing session, the research team will identify 10 to 15 key tasks for the users to perform.

The testing sessions are often measured in very quantitative terms, where the researchers try to measure the following:

- **Task Completion Rate and Average Completion Time:** How long does it take for users to complete tasks?

- **Task Efficiency Rate:** How many steps did it take for users to complete tasks? This data is compared or contrasted with the minimal number of steps required to complete that task.

- **UI Learnability Factor:** Does the learnability of a mobile site or application improve with repetition?

Don't confuse usability testing with focus group testing. Usability testing is quantitatively measured in a controlled environment to scientifically prove how well users can or cannot use a certain product.

Best Practices and Resources

The three main areas of mobile that are instrumental to any mobile project or marketing campaign are SMS text messaging, mobile site creation, and native application development. Each of these key areas continues to constantly evolve. As a result, keeping up to date on the latest changes in mobile is a challenge for designers and technologists. The following list of resources is a great starting point to keep designers and technologists abreast of all the latest developments in the world of mobile.

 ## SMS Resources

For those that need further background on best practices for executing SMS-based mobile marketing campaigns, the Mobile Marketing Association web site is a good place to start. The site is chock-full of industry case studies, white papers, and best practices. Also, learn about SMS best practices from the organization (CSCA) that administers short codes for all U.S. wireless carriers.

MOBILE MARKETING ASSOCIATION

On July 9, 2008, the Mobile Marketing Association (MMA) published the *Consumer Best Practices for Cross-Carrier Mobile Content Programs*. The PDF file can be downloaded from www. mmaglobal.com/bestpractices.pdf.

In the document, you will find guidelines for implementing short code programs, Interactive Voice Response (IVR), and off-deck mobile sites in the United States. The guidelines document is a compilation of accepted industry practices, wireless carrier policies, and regulatory guidance for the off-deck ecosystem. The guidelines document strives to implement policies that encourage the industry's growth via consumer protection and privacy.

COMMON SHORT CODE ADMINISTRATION (CSCA)

The CSCA administers for U.S. wireless carriers the common short codes that are used to address wireless messages. In addition, the CSCA oversees the technical and operational aspects of CSC functions and maintains a single database of available, reserved, and registered CSCs. The CSCA web site includes helpful insight into industry best practices.

www.usshortcodes.com/csc_best_practices.html

 ## Mobile Web

The mobile web is taking off and the venerable World Wide Web Consortium (W3C) is setting the pace for mobile site-construction guidelines. In addition, dev.mobi, dubbed the most exciting mobile development community, also provides great insight into mobile web development.

W3.ORG — MOBILE WEB BEST PRACTICES

The w3.org Mobile Web Best Practices document specifies best practices for delivering web content to mobile devices. The principal goal of the document is to improve the user experience when accessing the web from mobile devices.

www.w3.org/TR/2006/WD-mobile-bp-20060412/

DEV.MOBI

Touted as the world's most exciting mobile development community, dev.mobi features a robust Mobile Web Developer's Guide. The guide includes content tutorials about creating a mobile web strategy and mobile information architecture.

http://dev.mobi/content/mobile-web-developer%E2% 80%99s-guide-part-i

IPHONE

Check out the iPhone Web Development guidelines and learn the latest techniques on mobile browser–based design to ensure that you are designing the best user experience for your iPhone web applications.

http://developer.apple.com/webapps/

Native Application Development

iPhone, Google Android, Blackberry, Flash Lite, Symbian, J2ME, and widgets are all native application environments with different technical development environments and interface design guidelines. Trying to navigate each unique application environment is enough to drive designers and technologists mad. This section provides some great resources to learn how to kick-start content creation for different native application environments.

IPHONE NATIVE APPLICATION

Start from the horse's mouth. To design a compelling experience for your iPhone OS application, check out the Apple resource listed here.

http://developer.apple.com/iphone/library/navigation/Topics/ UserExperience/index.html

GOOGLE ANDROID

Begin developing Android applications with the same high-quality tools you would use to develop Java applications. The Android development tools make running, debugging, and testing your applications a snap.

http://code.google.com/android/devel/implementing-ui.html

LITTLE SPRINGS DESIGN—MOBILE DESIGN PATTERNS

Little Springs Design, a mobile-user-experience consulting group, provides free mobile UI design resources and patterns for the mobile design community via a wiki. The wiki's goal is to be the authoritative resource for all things related to the art and science of mobile-user-interface design.

http://patterns.littlespringsdesign.com/index.php/Main_Page

Conclusion

Mobile has an opportunity to be as large or larger than any other medium on the planet. The key statistic to keep in mind is 3.7 billion mobile phones on the planet: We have a built-in audience already to design and build for. As designers and technologists, we are challenged to create great mobile sites and applications that can be as technically complex as a web site builds. Therefore, for the mobile medium, the need to apply proper interaction design to our mobile projects is more important than ever before.

7

Visual Design

Visual design for mobile means dedication to the ever-evolving current trends and transitions in the handset industry. As the ability to display information at higher resolutions, sizes, and download times increases, so does the need for stronger visual design exploration. These opportunities often lead to progressive experiences that push this medium into new spaces.

A successful mobile design is one that communicates its content with simplicity and ease. It does not overpower the click stream of users' interaction paths. The design is courteous to users in its presentation, assuring a fast-loading and logical read. It safely accommodates the presentation and prioritization of information in the small-screen environment.

Establishing the Visual Phase

The visual design phase begins once the mobile interaction design has been completed. When moving into this phase, it is key that all parties involved understand the constraints posed. An overarching statement of good practice is "less is best." Quick loads and quick reads are a priority for the user audience. Anything that takes too long to load may cause users to lose interest and drop out of the experience.

As discussed in Chapter 5, knowing your target audience and knowing the multiple variables associated with its mobile environments (speed, carrier, and handsets) all play a very important role in visual design. Anything too visually complex may take too long to download. Certain carriers also place restrictions on areas of their screen spaces, so various dimensions need to be strictly abided by to assure all core content is visible in the display.

Only those handsets that can hop on WiFi, such as the Apple iPhone and iPod Touch, can support a heavier visual design experience. However, even with these designs there are visual constraints to abide by.

The Process

For the visual process to begin, a successful interaction design needs to have taken place along with a successful target audience analysis. The visual design team also examines if any other preexisting visual centers exist for the project. If a visual center currently exists in another communication channel (print, broadcast, web, or other), it should be carried over into the small screen and adapted accordingly. This way, users can experience a true multichannel journey and relate to cue points whether they are visual, content, or copy based.

DESIGNING TEMPLATES

Creating visuals for mobile is accomplished via templates, designed with defined recommendations and specifications based on the target audience analysis and interaction design. Just like in web design, the boards are developed as templates so that they can be populated with dynamic-based content when the development phase starts. Templates ensure a continuous theme as subsections of the experience are designed out.

Visual boards are developed in applications such as Adobe Photoshop and/or Adobe Illustrator. The dimensions of these boards are based on the target audience handsets. Best practice for designers is to aim for the highest dimension of their target audience. This goes for application-based mobile experience and mobile web experiences. The visual team will not only design for that highest size but also for all the smaller sizes. The "typical" target sizes are as follows:

- 480 × 320 @ 163 ppi (Apple iPhone)
- 320 × 240 @ 72 dpi (smart phone)
- 240 × 180 @ 72 dpi (medium handset)
- 176 × 128 @ 72 dpi (small handset)

The design template needs to be developed in a flexible manner that will allow it to port across handsets of other sizes. The designers must keep in mind that each handset has its own characteristics and user interfaces. Designs should not be developed from edge to edge; rather, they need to always consider the scrollbar and web browser. To be safe, always allow for an extra 10 pixels on the width (targeted width -10) and an extra 20 pixels on the height (targeted height -20).

All templates are produced in 8-bit RGB @ 72 dpi, with the exception of the iPhone, which is developed at 163 ppi. All original template boards are designed in true color, but most handsets do not support millions of colors, so the image color is reduced on the exports, as discussed later in this chapter.

COLOR OPTIMIZATION

Developing a color palette for a mobile project requires a lot of consideration. Mobile is a medium that can be viewed in all types of environments, from high noon to dusk. Every handset display has different bit depths and backlight strengths. The size dimensions of these displays places another variable into the mix. There is no perfect answer here, especially with the advancement of the handset market; however there are some safe guidelines to follow.

Vibrant, rich, primary colors typically display content with the most clarity, as they provide the highest contrast, even on the lower-end handsets. These colors are the most visible in most environmental conditions as well. Pastel colors and shades of grey tend to get lost in the display, especially on handsets that can't properly display true color tones due to a limited color-bit screen.

Any area of importance needs to utilize vibrant colors in order to attract users' attention. This could be anything from the content itself to the core interface design of headers, links, or buttons. These colors help separate it from the rest of the interface. See FIGURE 7.1.

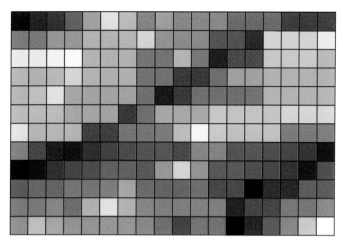

FIGURE 7.1 A sample color chart.

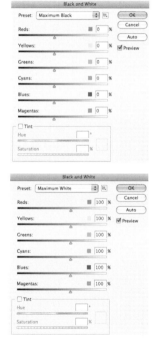

FIGURE 7.2 Optimizing black-and-white levels in Photoshop.

All nongraphical-based visuals should be designed in a manner that can easily be replicated in CSS (Cascading Style Sheets). A big feature of CSS for mobile is the ability to centralize the color scheme so that it can be shared among the various sizes of mobile framework templates. CSS covers attributes dealing with the font, colors, links, and so on. CSS also helps to reduce the overall page size.

PHOTOGRAPHIC IMAGE TREATMENT

In order to have a more vibrant appearance on the small screen, all photographic imagery should be adjusted to optimize the black-and-white levels and color tonality. See **FIGURE 7.2**. Finer detailed imagery may also require a slight "sharpening" effect in order to enhance some of its smaller details and present a crisper visual.

Photographic image sizes should stay within the confines of a target handset space. This avoids unnecessary scrolling and produces a more comfortable user experience.

Although photographic images in their original format are in millions of colors, these images are typically exported as JPG or PNG formats. During this process, much emphasis is placed on achieving the smallest potential file size. Handset screens are not capable of displaying true, rich colors, so exported images can take on a bit more compression—more than they would for desktop experiences. When these images are viewed on the lower-resolution handsets, the visible artifacting is barely noticeable. More compression means smaller file size, and smaller file size means a faster download. If you export out an image with a lower compression rate, users might not notice the difference because the handset cannot display the extra color information accurately.

When coding photographic images into place, the width and height need to be specified. Any missing information causes the handset to perform more and increases the render time.

TYPOGRAPHY TREATMENTS

There are two categories of typographic treatment for handsets:

1 Device fonts

2 Graphic fonts

Device fonts (see **FIGURE 7.3**) work in a similar way to system text (HTML font) on desktop web sites. They are limited to a select few fonts, depending on the device and platform. With the vast numbers of handsets on the market, these sets vary greatly, but a majority still support the basic Arial, Verdana, Helvetica, Default Sans, or Sans-Serif font collections. Device font is typically used for all body copy and any other areas that might be driven dynamically, such as headers, standard links, breadcrumb trails, and so on. This is true for both application-based and mobile web experiences.

ARIAL
The Quick Brown Fox Jumps Over The Lazy Dog.

HELVETICA
The Quick Brown Fox Jumps Over The Lazy Dog.

TIMES
The Quick Brown Fox Jumps Over The Lazy Dog.

VERDANA
The Quick Brown Fox Jumps Over The Lazy Dog.

FIGURE 7.3 Device fonts.

Graphical-based fonts (see **FIGURE 7.4**) are those used when a design calls for a special typographic treatment, such those found in headers, titles, or branding. In these instances, the typographic layouts are produced in Adobe Photoshop or Adobe Illustrator and then exported out as a flat graphic. These files are typically exported out as either PNGs or GIFs.

BERTHOLD AKZIDENZ GROTESK BE EXTRA BOLD
THE QUICK BROWN FOX JUMPS OVER THE LAZY DOG.

HELVETICA NEUE BOLD
THE QUICK BROWN FOX JUMPS OVER THE LAZY DOG.

TRADE GOTHIC BOLD
THE QUICK BROWN FOX JUMPS OVER THE LAZY DOG.

STANDARD
The Quick Brown Fox Jumps Over The Lazy Dog.

FIGURE 7.4 Graphic fonts.

If the mobile experience is more of an application-based project, the font set can be embedded into the build, allowing the fonts to be dynamically printed in the desired typeface as necessary. With the mobile web, this is not possible. A mobile web site can only access system-based fonts installed on users' handsets, much like how a desktop HTML experience works. If the design of the mobile web page requires a specific typographic treatment, it must be exported out as graphical assets and implemented into the build.

FIGURE 7.5 Adobe Flash Lite applications.

Self-contained applications, such as those created in Adobe Flash Lite (see **FIGURE 7.5**) and Java, allow for more flexibility in the visual design and use of typography. Select fonts can be embedded in these applications to adhere to a project's visual center. However, since these mobile projects are ones that users must download and install, ensure the file size is conservative, as it will live on their handsets until they delete it. Prime examples of these types of applications are games and branded utilities, such as banking applets.

Font sizes of 6 to 10 points are often used, depending on the font family. Mono-spaced, pixel-based fonts often work best, as they provide the sharpest contrast. Anti-aliased fonts are also an option, but must be selectively chosen. Anything that is too stylized may render poorly on select handset displays. Typographic families that take on more square-based properties are often the best choice, as there is a clear character definition at smaller resolutions.

Iconography is often associated with typography. Iconography is any image or logo treatment that represents an idea, such as the placement of a video camera graphic or a film still graphic (which signifies the idea of a "movie file"). In the small screen, user interface elements such as iconography must be strong enough for the viewer to recognize or understand at first glance. Any element that is not interpretable upon first glance must either be perfected or avoided in order to preserve a fluid read. Strong iconic treatments are the ones that users are accustomed to in their experiences. They immediately communicate their purpose without question.

Any icons associated with navigation, headers, or content must be positioned immediately alongside (or "locked up" with) its corresponding content. If you don't consider smaller handset screens, icons and text might wrap, thus disassociating the icon with the text. With the text and image separated, this may appear as two separate links to the user and present a break in communication. To eliminate this potential problem, safely lock up icons with their associated blocks of content. See **Figure 7.6**.

Figure 7.6 Common graphic icon and text lockup.

COPY TREATMENTS

Copy and calls to action within the mobile space should be clear and concise to mobile users of all levels. Excessive reading on a small screen is just added information and should be avoided where possible. Keeping the copy succinct allows for digestible content and keeps users interested. Techie terms, buzzwords, and acronyms related to the mobile space should be avoided; these often confuse and disassociate users with the experience. Disclaimers and other related items should be written in a simple, easy to understand manner.

As good practice, copy should accompany all media types and/or anything that will trigger an action or response, such as forms, SMS windows, and so on. Association with any file size, file format, downloads, and/or services such as MMS represents a courtesy that users appreciate. Users may quickly leave a site experience if they find what they click is not what they want. Describing what they will see prior to clicking keeps users on a steady, interactive path.

When displaying copy on a page, it's typically best to print large body text as black text against a white background or white text against a black background. This preserves the contrast and allows a much more fluid read for users. Any other color palette combinations may not render as clearly and cause difficulty in the read.

Page Layout and Navigation

"Above the fold" is a graphic design concept commonly associated with print- and desktop-based web projects. This refers to the space immediately visible in the upper portion of a page, such as the portion of a newly loaded web page in a browser window that you can see without scrolling. Any content that is not visible upon first load and is considered "offscreen" is said to be "below the fold." To access this "below the fold" content, one must scroll the page. This concept still holds true in the mobile space, but with even more of a reduced viewing area. See FIGURE 7.7.

All core navigation, branding, breadcrumbs, messaging, and core content should be visible "above the fold" in a mobile experience. Not only does this signal to users the primary area of focus, but from a strategic standpoint, the mobile device keypad tabs through these items in the order of top-left of the page to the bottom-right of the page. Core priority navigation items or features in the top space ensure quick ease of access for users, thus getting them into the experience faster.

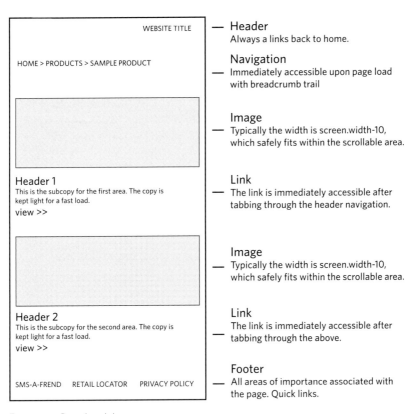

FIGURE 7.7 Page breakdown.

Standardization in the user interface and a constant visual reference in your navigation allow the user to quickly jump to menu items with ease. Re-inventing navigation on a mobile device only confuses the user. Standardization provides simplicity, and simplicity provides longer user explorations.

All clickable items should have a clear navigational element or reference icon to illustrate that they are navigational elements. When developing any type of link on the page, the preference is to keep it as a hypertext link that is easily accessible by users.

The header area of a mobile experience typically rests in the upper 20 to 30 pixels of the layout. As a common practice, the header is typically linkable back to the index or main page of an application. Headers should be treated distinctively from user interface elements so users can scan pages with ease. Excessive headers and graphical horizontal lines often break users' ability to read on a small screen and should be kept to a minimum.

The header is typically followed by one of three items:

1 A breadcrumb trail, which represents a clickable path to where the user has visited

2 Core navigation for the experience

3 A branded lead image that establishes the presence of the experience

These items are interchangeable in their positions, but all provide a quick access point of click at the top of the page. Navigation can be either horizontal or vertical depending on how the screen real estate is divided out in the interaction design. The navigation should be clear to the user in a visual sense and not graphically heavy. The buttons should stand out on the page with clearly formatted text, whether they are graphical- or device-based fonts. Users must be able to scan the navigation once and clearly understand all the options. As users navigate a project, the breadcrumb trail should populate with each link that has been accessed. This allows users to click back to a previous experience with ease.

All mobile handsets have unique browsers, versions of browsers, and sizes of browsers. The same handset on different carriers may have different browsers. This means that when laying out a page, all core areas of focus need to be immediately accessible, viewable, and understandable upon first glance. Some mobile browsers are not clear with their forward/back functionality, so the previous items should be built into the experience to assist users with their journeys.

The main body area of a site should consist of the core content, but there are restrictions to the length of this area. Testing proves that select handset makes have trouble displaying pages with long body-format content. These handsets and browsers truncate the content in mid-layout. Formatting information and pagination can get around this. Keep in mind that the small-screen mobile experience should be direct and trimmed down. This does not mean you should lose the depth of the content or message, but you should lose the excess that is not needed.

The footer area is another key area of the page. It is an area reserved for cross-experience functionality, such as SMS-to-a-Friend, Privacy Policy, About, Legal, and so on. It is a persistent navigation across the experience. By placing these in the footer, it separates the excessive content from the core content. Each has its corresponding page, separate from the core experience. A "Back to Top" may also be found in the footer, allowing users to jump back up to the top of the page layout.

By placing SMS-to-a-Friend in the footer, you provide users with constant access points so they can forward the experience to their friends. This button typically links to a form on a corresponding page or on the page itself, where users can type their friends' mobile numbers and submit. The outgoing text message can be controlled, to ensure the correct information is delivered.

Integrating Content Media Types

Integrating media types, such as audio and video, can be extremely beneficial to any mobile project, whether it is a mobile web site, application, or Bluetooth experience. Just like with all audio/video projects, it is the content itself that makes the piece impactful, not just the fact that it is audio or video.

Within the mobile space, the use of audio and video has to be done with absolute attention to the target audience, their carriers, and their handsets. If the files are too large, or incompatible, or noncompliant with carrier standards, the mobile project can result in an unpleasant user experience. If users do not have a data plan capable of supporting larger data transfers, they may also end up with a heavy mobile bill at the end of the month.

Video

Mobile video integration (see **Figure 7.8**) takes on the same practices as online desktop video, but with even more precision. Video containing a lot of movement requires more data to compress; more data means staggering downloads and poor playback performance on select handsets. Not all video is suitable for mobile due to the compression that it needs to go through prior to integration. Videos containing the least camera movement and minimal in-frame camera movement render the best quality at the lowest file size.

Figure 7.8 Mobile video.

Video with a higher contrast compresses much better than video with multiple shades and/or gradients. Colors in the red and orange spectra are often a bit more difficult to work with because they require more data to portray accurately. These colors tend to bleed without sufficient data allocation. Expect to see higher file sizes with these colors present.

Since video content varies, there is no universal compression practice to achieve the best compression or quality. Proper video compression settings are determined on a per-video basis. However, a core set of established compression settings are used as the base configuration and adjusted as needed. Settings are adjusted based on the length of the video, colors within the video, target handset makes, and the amount of frame movement. See **FIGURE 7.9**.

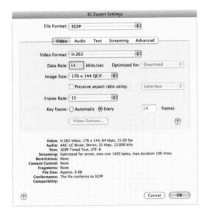 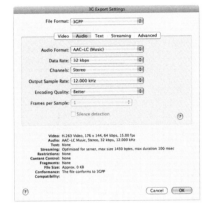

FIGURE 7.9 Compression settings within the Media Cleaner application.

PREPRODUCTION PROCESS

The preproduction process for bringing video into the mobile environment is as follows:

1 Capture the video into an application such as Apple Final Cut Pro.

2 Perform the necessary edits.

3 Export the video as Fullframe Uncompressed QuickTime.

4 Import the video into an application such as Adobe After Effects and adjust the contrast and curve settings so that blacks are an absolute black value and whites are an absolute white value. Finesse the colors tones as needed.

5 Render out the video as a Fullframe Uncompressed QuickTime.

6 Import the video into a compression program, such as Adobe QuickTime Pro or Media Cleaner.

At this stage, the video is optimized to its extent in terms of color and contrast. All unnecessary gradients or light bursts should now be minimized or removed.

Knowing the target audience's handsets and the properties of those handsets are an important step in setting the compression settings. What type of video do the handsets support? What size dimensions? Is streaming supported by a majority of the carriers? Do the carriers support downloads? If not, what do they receive?

Once this information is known, sample settings such as those in the following section may be applied as a base.

COMPRESSION SETTINGS

Compression is not completed upon one pass. The compressionist should prepare to render a handful of variants based on the following, and all should be tested locally for visual quality. Once the visual quality is approved, playback tests are performed whereby the files are placed on a server and the targeted handsets are tested with this media.

Standard Base WAP reference settings include:

- **Final Output Format:** 3gp. 3gp stands for Third Generation Partnership Project. It is a multimedia container format and a simplified version of MP4, which is optimized for mobile in terms of decreased storage and bandwidth requirements. Most GSM-based phones utilize the .3gp file format, which supports a larger percentage of the mobile audience.

- **Video Format:** H.263. A majority of handsets are safely capable of displaying the H.263 format, which is a video codec (compressor-decompressor). A small percentage of handsets are capable of supporting H.264, but present a limitation to the larger audience.

- **Video KBS:** 50 kbs to 120 kbs (target audience dependent). The unit of measurement equal to 1024 bytes. The higher the kb rate the better the picture quality in a compressed file. Most mobile video compressions require a lower number as suggested in the above numbers, to maintain optimal play-back performance, as well as a smaller file size.

- **FPS:** 15 frames per second. Video typically runs at 29.97 frames per second.

- **Key Frame:** Every 24 frames (Real-time Transport Protocol, or RTP). In the data stream, this is where a complete image is stored. If a lag occurs in the video playback, the stream will jump to this frame and continue to play. The more key frames present in a compressed video, the higher the file size may be.

- **Audio Compression:** AAC (Advanced Audio Coding). This is typically used for audio recordings that contain both voice and sound. AMR (Adaptive Multi-Rate) is another option that is typically used for audio recordings composed of only speech.

- **Audio Data Rate:** 10–50 kb (target audience dependent). The higher the data rate, the better the quality. With mobile, one needs to consider that the audio is coming through a handset speaker and does not require the highest data rates. Details of individual projects also dictate the emphasis or need for prioritizing accompanying music and/or sound.

- **Audio Sample Rate:** 12 khz. The higher the kilohertz rate the better the audio quality, but with the acknowledgement that most handsets will not be able to accurately play back higher-end audio formats.

- **Hinting Method:** Keyframe. Hinting allows for a more seam-less video playback. By setting to keyframe, the video can jump to the next keyframe when a lag arises.

- **Optimized for Streaming:** True (when applicable and deployed from a streaming server, such as Akamai).

- **Maximum Packet Size:** 1450 bytes.

- **Maximum Packet Duration:** 100 millisecond.

If the project's target audience also contains Windows Smart Phone users, the video will need to be encoded in WMV format to support those handsets. The same rules apply as those previously listed, with the exception of tailoring to the Windows format. The Apple iPhone also has its own format (MP4), which allows for a bit more generosity in terms of colors, compression, and audio formats.

If the video is run from a local app, chances are this video still needs to stream into the handset or be downloaded. However, these files might benefit from a little extra data applied to boost appearance quality, so the above settings might fluctuate slightly.

Users should be given the option to either download a media file or stream the file when streaming is made available within a project:

- Downloading allows users to save the media file to their handsets. Downloading is dependent on having a mobile carrier that allows downloads and also a handset that has enough storage space to save the downloaded files.

- Streaming transmits data over users' mobile connections as they engage with the content. Streaming does not retain the file. Streaming is dependent on having a mobile carrier that allows streaming media to its handsets as well as the necessary software to allow an RTSP (Real Time Streaming Protocol) connection. RTSP allows for time-based access to files that live on the server via a remote client. Streaming requires that you perform additional testing to assure quality in the playback and stream. Additional costs are typically associated with streaming-media-based projects to cover the additional server setup fees and streaming bandwidth.

When working with media clips, a thumbnail should always be present to act as a preview to the user. This acts as a courtesy, since most mobile data connections are not at very high speed. Users gain a better understanding of the clip before they proceed to download or stream the media. Downloading media can take a long time; if users download a clip that they ultimately didn't want to view, it proves to be a failed experience. See **Figure 7.10**.

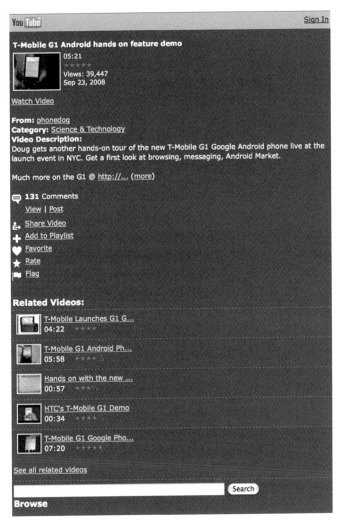

FIGURE 7.10 This focus is on media thumbnail and size relationships.

When text is locked up alongside the thumbnail, the thumbnail should be approximately one-third the handset width. Larger thumbnails can also be effective, but they will increase the page size and download time. These larger thumbnails often take the full width of the screen, giving users a larger preview of what they are about to download.

Audio

When audio is compressed on its own, it follows the same standards as when it is compressed with video, except with closer attention to details and quality. Not all handsets support the same variant of audio compression, and if the purpose of the file is specifically for this reason, the correct version needs to be served up. Certain handsets also have limitations on the length of ringtones, so once the files are created, thorough testing needs to take place. Various forms of the same file need to be served up to accommodate the wide range of specifications. These types of files are typically downloaded or delivered via MMS.

- **Final Output Format:** When audio is served up separately as a ringtone or music file, the file should be exported out in three formats: WAV, MIDI, and MP3. Audio support on handsets varies greatly, so with proper handset detection in place users should be served up the corresponding format for their devices.

- **Audio Compression:** AAC or AMR. AAC stands for Advanced Audio Coding and is typically used for audio recordings that contain both voice and sound. AMR (Adaptive Multi-Rate) is another option, which is typically used for audio recordings composed of just speech.

- **Audio Data Rate:** 10–50 kb (target audience dependent). The higher the data rate, the better the quality. With mobile, one needs to consider that the audio is coming through a handset speaker and does not require the highest of data rates. Details of individual projects also dictate the emphasis/need for prioritizing accompanying music and/or sound.

- **Audio Sample Rate:** 12 khz. The higher the kilohertz rate the better the audio quality, but with the acknowledgment that most handsets will not be able to accurately play back higher-end audio formats.

Conclusion

Once all of the visual designs have been completed per the process detailed in this chapter, and all the media assets have been prepped, the visual team begins to slice and export out imagery for the technical phase. This is similar to the production process in web design. Because many of these users will be viewing or downloading content via a standard mobile data plan, it's important to use the smallest possible file size. Every page of a mobile web experience is calculated in data size—down to the code itself (which also needs to be optimized). If the project is an application-based experience, certain handsets have limited disk space to work with, so every kb is important. Truly knowing the target audience and their handsets drives both the visual phase and the asset preparation phase of a mobile project.

8

Pioneering Tools for Mobile Development and Services

Name: Michael Becker

Occupation: EVP of Business Development, Founder of iLoop Mobile

Device: Uses the Nokia N71 as his main devices, and is looking forward to the upcoming release of the BlackBerry Bold.

Mobile Data Habits: Consumes mobile data on a daily basis; surfs mobile sites to look for information; directions, and/or details on a company; uses Google Maps 10 to 15 times a week when searching for directions. Almost never uses downloadable applications and, if so, uses these applications approximately two to three times and then never uses them again. On average, sends approximately 10 to 20 text messages per day.

Background

Michael Becker is a leader in the mobile marketing industry, taking on the roles of industry practitioner, industry volunteer, and entrepreneurial academic. Michael is co-founder and EVP of Business Development at iLoop Mobile, Inc., a leading mobile marketing platform solutions provider and winner of the Mobile Marketing Association (MMA) Innovation of the Year Award (2007).

Michael sits on the MMA's North American board of directors and global board of directors, founded co-chairs the award winning MMA's Academic Outreach Committee and founded and co-edits the award winning MMA International Journal of Mobile Marketing, the world's only academic journal focused on the use of the mobile channel for marketing. Michael is also a member of the DotMobi Mobile Advisory Group Steering Committee and is a member of the U.S. Direct Marketing Association mobile council.

In addition to his practitioner and industry roles, Michael is a contributing author to Mobile Internet for Dummies, is co-author of Web Marketing All-in-One Desk Reference For Dummies, has authored over 40 articles on mobile marketing, oversees an industry blog and is pursing his doctorate on the topic of mobile enhanced customer managed interactions. In recognition of his contributions to the industry, Michael was awarded the MMA Individual Achievement Award in 2007.

See **Figures 8.1** through **8.3**.

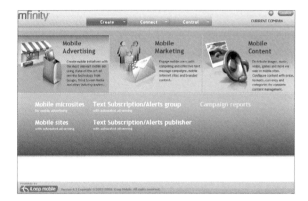

Figure 8.1 iLoop's award-winning mFinity platform: Users can utilize this platform to create and manage their SMS campaigns and mobile web sites, and also manage their content distribution.

Figure 8.2 The mFinity platform provides quick and easy creation of mobile Internet sites with a user-friendly, drag-and-drop interface. There is almost zero coding required to launch a basic mobile web site.

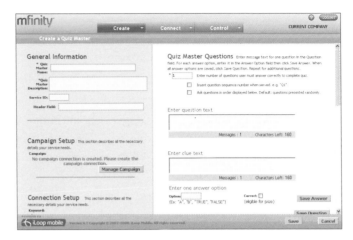

Figure 8.3 mFinity's easy-to-use templates to create, launch, and manage any type of SMS-related programs that you can imagine.

Interview

AUTHORS: How long have you worked in mobile, and what was your first mobile project?

MB: I've been involved with the mobile industry since 1996.

The first project I was involved with was in international business development for Hewlett-Packard, where we built satellite-handset test systems. I worked in this area for approximately 2.5 years.

I then worked in an electronic books company shortly thereafter. My main responsibility was managing the content distribution system of electronic books to handheld devices via the Internet. Through this, I learned how to deliver content via WiFi and related mobile radio technologies. I also worked on the ability to make purchases via a dedicated mobile electronic book.

In 1999, I worked on instant messaging software for mobile operator networks. This software was capable of delivering images/video via a downloadable client on the mobile phone (Palm/SmartPhones). I also began to explore some of the first WAP-based solutions during this time.

Shortly after this, I went on to start my doctorate. During my doctorate studies, I began to develop a mobile marketing company and eight months later I found some people to start up iLoop Mobile.

AUTHORS: Your company, iLoop Mobile, provides tools for brands, content creators, agencies, and enterprises to launch SMS and mobile site projects quickly and effectively. In your opinion, what are some of the major industry hurdles around creating content for mobile?

MB: Literacy is the first major industry hurdle, similar to the beginning of the HTML world. It was a mystery at first, but then the industry realized it was not that difficult. It is the learning curve of overcoming this through the agency and marketer's knowledge of how to do it.

 www.mmaglobal.com/modules/article/view.article.php/74

The second hurdle is the misunderstanding that the mobile phone is not only limited to one channel. There are multiple channels within this space—SMS, MMS, email, Bluetooth, voice, mobile Internet, and downloadable applications. Each channel has its own adoption rate and usage curves amongst the target audiences. Unfortunately, most marketers see mobile as being one single channel, as opposed to seeing mobile as being different channels with various levels of maturity.

AUTHORS: There's a lot of buzz these days around mobile applications. Why would brands and content creators choose creating mobile applications over creating a mobile web site?

MB: Today, my answer would be they choose to do so because they are following the mainstream buzz. These groups may not truly understand why they are creating mobile applications at the present time, but they realize that in four to five years, this will serve as a main channel. This exploration educates the brands and content creators as they experiment with niche markets and help determine if their audiences are actually using the applications.

A good rule to remember is if you don't know your audience's handset, you should assume the majority of your audience does not know how to use an application or have data plans that support it. According to recent mMetrics data, only 10 percent of mobile users have an unlimited data plan and 25 percent have any form of recognizable data plan tied to their phone.

Users also often forget that they've downloaded a mobile application. The user also has to go through the process of manually locating and launching the application each time they wish to engage with it. The average mass market consumer will not know how to use a downloadable mobile application. Network carriers also play an important role in the downloadable application world. For instance, certain carriers prevent automatic feeds being pulled into the application.

If the target audience is a BlackBerry or iPhone user, the downloadable application makes sense—mass market solution dictates. An example would be the Weather Channel for the BlackBerry, Google Maps, and so on. These brands know their audience's devices.

AUTHORS: Do you ever envision the mobile world following the same evolution path as the web? More standardized and easier to launch sites and applications for the masses?

MB: There is no question that at some point in the future this will happen. The question is more about what will end up slowing down or speeding up that process. Potential blockers could be carriers wanting to control the pipe. Mobile is not the Internet—it is a controlled pipe. Individual entities can slow down or speed up the pipe based on their view and what they want the world to be like. How do they work within this space and grow within this space?

There is also no standard operating system present in the mobile world, unlike the PC, Mac, and Linux of the desktop world. Symbian, Traditional, Android, Brew, Linux, Windows, Palm, and Apple are the current mobile platforms. A dedicated device versus conversion device poses additional challenges that need to be accounted for.

You will see much faster standardization on how the content is accessed and managed versus how it is actually displayed (Web 2.0, content mashup, mechanisms of standardizing).

AUTHORS: What are you excited about these days with regards to the mobile industry?

MB: I'm excited about a lot richer, smarter phones, dedicated phones, the streamlined structuring of data, both legacy broadband and Web 2.0 data. There are quite a few varying levels of display and rendering techniques—a lot of location relevance to this data as well.

You will also see a model for consumer-controlled Personal Identifiable Information and non–Personal Identifiable Information. PII and non-PII will significantly influence how brands will interact with individuals. The mobile channel will be a significant mode of communication for this new method of marketing.

AUTHORS: Fast-forward five years into the future: Can you paint me a picture of the mobile world?

MB: Mobile has become mainstreamed. Everyone has a phone. From a global market perspective, the primary form of communication is the mobile phone, such as those found in the current emerging markets of China and India. The mobile phone has become the remote control of our lives. We'll use mobile as the primary mode of communication, but if we're near another mode, such as a desktop PC, we'll utilize that.

This concept is recognized by marketers, so let's figure out how to reach the audiences. Let's educate ourselves now and figure this out. In the past, marketers would expect the mobile companies to provide free access to these tools, but there is now recognition that they must invest in them.

We're moving out of the realm of "pay someone to do this for me" to "I am now ready to license the tools to learn how to do it myself," and/or recognize that I need to pay someone to do this for me in a repeatable, consistent manner utilizing standardized tools. When you start leveraging tools, and a consistent set of tools based on standards, this allows for a comparison of the success rate versus delivery rate with predictable cost structures and timelines. Standardization eliminates the problem commonly encountered in the past, where 5 to 15 mobile partners utilized over the course of time caused problems with inconsistent reporting, inconsistent structure(s), and inconsistent methodologies. It makes the comparing and ROI analysis of the initiatives extremely difficult for apples-to-apples comparison.

User-generated content is also going to play a much bigger role in the future of mobile. Content becomes uncontrollable. The question then becomes, "Who is going to say who is legally liable?" and "Who is going to police the content?" The legal liability associated with porn, hate, and so on, is an issue, and we're seeing that laws are maturing much slower than the technology of the market.

AUTHORS: Any last words of inspiration for the creatives, designers, and developers working in the mobile industry?

MB: Mobile is totally approachable and completely doable. The key is to think Marketing 101:

- Who is my audience?

- How do I reach them?

- What devices do they have?

- What networks are they on?

- What value is my audience looking for?

The answers derived from these questions provide the necessary delivery methods and services. If you are serving a mass market audience, text messaging is the prime example.

Creatives should understand that the mobile channel is here and viable. There are a wide range of approaches, such as voice, text, mobile Internet, and downloadable applications. One must make sure to set expectations appropriately on how successful one channel may be over another. There are various mechanisms in getting data to the device or getting the individual to interact with the device.

However, creatives need to also take into consideration issues like standardization, both from a business and technical sense. The recognition that just because the feature is on the phone doesn't necessarily mean the consumer knows how to use it. A current MMA study states that the average consumer only knows how to use 4.7 features on their phone versus 10 to 20 features that are available on the phone.

Lastly, be totally excited about the mobile channel. Realize that not only is it the wave of the future, but a primary mode of communication for the masses. We have to recognize the limitation of mass markets and niche markets along with potential future market capability.

9

Location-Based Mobile Shopping

Name: Alex Muller

Occupation: Founder, CEO, Slifter

Device: Uses an iPhone to demo Slifter because it looks the best, and uses a BlackBerry for real work.

Mobile Data Habits: Consumes mobile content that includes SMS, mobile web, and native applications very often. Has about 40 phones at work, so consuming mobile data pretty often may be an understatement.

Background

Slifter is an online, mobile service/application that helps consumers find and share good shopping deals on the Web or on the phone. By using local product data feeds supplied by retailers, Slifter provides an innovative, web-based, mobile-shopping experience to users. No matter where you are or whenever it is, Slifter allows consumers to search for items and find good deals. Users can use their mobile phones to search via wireless web or use Slifter's proprietary Java download. Consumers can also use text messaging to find prices and availability simply by texting a product name, model number, and ZIP code to the predetermined Slifter short code. **FIGURES 9.1** and **9.2** show Slifter product images.

FIGURE 9.1 Slifter locates a product for you and points you to a retailer that has the product in stock.

FIGURE 9.2 Screenshots of the Slifter service via mobile site and as a proprietary Java download. Search for any product by ZIP code.

Interview

AUTHORS: How long have you worked in mobile, and what was your first mobile project?

AM: I've been working in mobile for three and a half years, which is quite a while now. First project was Slifter Beta, which was a J2ME MIDP1.0 application that was under 64 kilobytes.

AUTHORS: Your company, Slifter, is a company that utilizes location-based technologies to connect consumers with local retail stores. In your opinion, where is GPS heading within mobile, and how valuable is GPS to a consumer's experience while using mobile services?

AM: We believe GPS is extremely valuable. For one reason, it provides convenience and context. So one thing that a lot of people ask me is why mobile is really different from the Internet? And I think GPS-location awareness is one of the key differentiators. It can't really be stressed enough that the context of usage is what really makes mobile different. Not so much that the screen is just smaller, but it's what you do with it and what you're planning to do. And I think one of the things that you'll see from Slifter usage is that the location aspect is important because most of Slifter usage is on the street when you're out and about. So I think GPS is very important. Now we refer to it as GPS, but I also want to say that we're not really tied to satellite technology, whether it's cell-powered triangulation or reading Wi-Fi hotspots—it's some way of making the phone aware of its location.

AUTHORS: Have consumers been quick to adopt or demand GPS-based services and applications?

AM: I actually think GPS in our case is nice to have because people looking for local shopping information would rather not have to input in their ZIP codes. I think in the U.S., ZIP codes have been actually pretty convenient for mobile because it is a five-digit numeric entry. But obviously if you go abroad, they don't really have that system, so GPS is a must because to input on your mobile device an entire city and street address is very cumbersome.

On the flip side, I think that there are certain applications on mobile where it is extremely important. However, it's also a question of resolution. We consider ourselves a low-resolution application. We don't need to know where a user is standing within 50 feet; we only need to know where they are standing within 1,000 feet.

AUTHORS: Your service Slifter was one of the first in the mobile industry to support mobile shopping and commerce. Where do you think mobile commerce currently is in its life cycle? When do you predict it will become an "acceptable" means for commerce?

AM: It really depends how we define mobile commerce. So, Slifter is a mobile, local shopping solution. It really helps you find products at local stores. It's really not about ship-to-home retail. And what I mean by that is, we don't believe that anyone is using their mobile phone to buy an HDTV that they're going to ship to their home from a mobile phone. Also, I don't think it's about the technology. It's not that technology isn't there to support that—it is, actually. It's the fact that, why would a consumer want to use a two-inch screen for something they're going to receive three to five days later? For Slifter it's about in-store pickup. I think Fandango mobile is an excellent example of in-store pickup. It's a service where I can buy movie tickets wherever I am. So if I'm at a restaurant and decide on what movie I want to watch while I'm eating dinner, I can then put in my order via my mobile device. I'll make the ticket purchase and then I'll use my credit card to pick it up when I'm at the venue. We are strong believers that that is one of the mechanisms that will drive what will be considered mobile commerce because right now, many famous click-and-mortar web sites you know, some of the big names, will tell you that 25 percent of their e-commerce is actually driving in-store pickup.

AUTHORS: Your service, Slifter, is also available as a proprietary mobile application, and it has been for a few years now. However, just recently there's been a lot of buzz around mobile applications. Why would brands and content creators choose creating mobile applications over creating mobile web sites?

AM: This is an interesting question. We get this question a lot. Is the answer native application or is it mobile web site? My answer is, it depends—but for Slifter we actually do both.

Native applications will always have advantages for certain kinds of things over mobile web sites. For instance, native applications can seamlessly integrate into a mobile device's contact list capabilities, GPS, and camera technology. You can also do a lot more lower-level development with a native application. Native applications can also take better advantage of a phone's memory. Wireless networks are getting faster, but latency is still a problem, so a native application can do things with streaming data that a mobile web site can't do.

Now, on the flip side, if you're somebody like Slifter, you can't launch without a mobile web site for several reasons. Mobile web sites give you organic traffic. Mobile web sites let you have a catchall for mobile handsets you haven't deployed a native application for. There really is a set of users that prefers to get to know your service on a mobile web site before they download it to their mobile device.

From our perspective, it's not about native application versus mobile web site. It's A) Do you need to have access to local features on your phone, such as GPS, contact list, or camera phone integration? In which case, you don't have a choice, and you must create a native application. Or B) Can you use both to say I'm going to use a mobile web site to let the consumers get familiar with my mobile service, and then once they become a fan, I'm going to let them download the native application because downloaded applications see a lot more retention and more prominent usage.

AUTHORS: Where is your application currently available for download?

AM: Anybody can point their mobile device to Slifter.com for download, and we'll do device detection to serve you the most appropriate download for your device. We have a BlackBerry version and a J2ME version. Additionally, Slifter is available as a download from the Nokia platform, and you can download it now from the Sprint deck and from several other decks. What's interesting is the Slifter mobile web site is also available on various Tier One decks from carriers.

AUTHORS: In your opinion who (handset OEM or carrier) do you think is doing the best job at evolving the mobile application landscape?

AM: There's no doubt in almost everybody's mind that the iPhone has done tremendous things for exploring new capacities for mobile applications. I'm a believer as well. However, one thing that I will say is that you also need to give credit to BlackBerry and Nokia because they shouldn't be underestimated. Nokia probably has one of the most solid development environments for mobile application development, whether it's for J2ME or for Symbian. I also want to point out that for the BlackBerry, there are elements of developing for BlackBerry such as contact list and GPS integration that are very efficient. So I think iPhone takes the top prize because it's really a platform that you can build this next-generation interface around. But BlackBerry and Nokia are really strong as well.

AUTHORS: On the topic of applications and everything that you've been doing with your product, what would you say is probably one of the biggest challenges in development. Would you say it's the actual development itself, porting, or the QA process?

AM: The biggest challenge is porting. And I think porting is a challenge, but I think porting has gotten actually a lot more complicated because porting now does not only mean porting from Java to Brew, it also might mean porting the design specifically for the varying mobile devices out there.

AUTHORS: Fast-forward five years into the future: Can you paint me a picture of the mobile world?

AM: I think that we're going to see a proliferation of even more devices. For instance, every time there's a new style of device, it doesn't really cancel the previous style. As you see, the iPhone's here, but people still like the form factor of a smaller BlackBerry, and some people still like clamshells, and some people like these tiny little devices. I think that one of the most complicated pieces here is that you're not porting from Brew to Java, but you're also porting from device to device, and you're porting from device context to device context. So I think all these devices are going to have 3G-to-4G network capabilities. In fact, right now, I can show you a Sprint LX LG 400. It's got a 128 x 160 wide screen, yet it's got 3G download rates. So here you've got a tiny screen and you've got 3G and GPS on this little device.

It's not so much that you're designing for the iPhone. It's the fact that the iPhone user is a little bit different than a Motorola V9 user in how they use their mobile application. I think a lot of iPhone users will use their iPhone Wi-Fi-enabled while they're sitting at home.

As an application designer, you want to understand the context for each. It doesn't mean you shouldn't develop an application on the Motorola RAZR on the new ones because they also have fast data speeds and a really crystal-clean, crystal-clear display. It just means that you might have to think about the application a little differently.

AUTHORS: Do you have any last words of inspiration for the creative designers and developers working in the mobile industry?"

AM: I don't know about words of inspiration, but I'll try my best. We'll start with "the industry's complex." There are a lot of large companies in the mobile industry, and it's a little bit different than, say, when the Internet was just starting out. I think this industry has the big handset manufacturers and the big carriers as major companies, and they also have the smaller startups and content creators as a different kind of company. And what's interesting is that they both need each other. As you're looking at these new devices that are coming out, the major companies are expecting that entrepreneurial companies are going to create applications and services to facilitate use for that device.

So as a smaller company looking to create services and applications, you're not going to get Nokia, Apple, and Verizon to bend to what you want to do, and they're each probably going to go in a different direction even for the next five years. And I don't think if you want to be in this game you can go into it hoping a standard emerges, because it won't. Each of these companies have their own strategic plans, and yet they think about the ecosystem in general, but they each feel they're big enough for their own ecosystem, and they probably are.

So given these are massive companies with a lot of pull, each potentially pulling in different directions, I think designers and developers have to be very flexible, and you have to make a lot of decisions on how you design and build out your services and applications. I think the best way to make that decision is to understand the context of what you're trying to do.

You know, in Slifter's case, we're trying to be a ubiquitous local shopping tool. So with that kind of thought, then we understand the path in front of us. We want to make it as easy to put Slifter on your phone as possible, and make it as sticky as possible. But if you're doing something different, if your use case is something different, you might want to make a different decision. And I think that's something that every application developer should realize. Lastly, and this is probably the inspirational part, because it is a complex landscape, because it's fragmented in many cases, there's an opportunity to create really interesting solutions that do create a lot of wealth.

10

Connecting the Physical with Virtual

Name: Stan Wiechers

Occupation: Partner in Brothers of Invention, LLC, and cofounder of Semapedia.org

Device: Nokia N95

Mobile Data Habits: Either text messages or surfs the mobile web every 30 minutes.

Background

Stan Wiechers is a mobile industry veteran and partner in his company, Brothers of Invention (http://brothers-of-invention. com/), a creative technology agency specializing in establishing connections between the real world and mobile Internet services. Some of his more notable projects are Semapedia.org (www.semapedia.org), TigTags.com (www.tigtags.com), and Video Meets Function (http://videomeetsfunction.com/).

Semapedia.org is a nonprofit, community-driven project that Stan helped found in September 2005. See **Figure 10.1**. The project's main goal is to connect the virtual world with the physical world by bringing the right information from the Internet to a user's mobile device in the physical world. Semapedia.org is also an open platform that allows the world to collaboratively hyperlink their physical world with the virtual world.

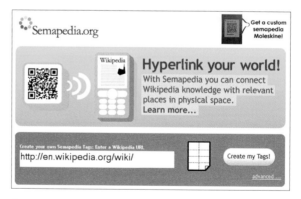

Figure 10.1 Semapedia.org is an open platform that allows the world to collaboratively hyperlink their physical world with the virtual world.

Semapedia Tags (see **Figure 10.2**) can be created directly on the Semapedia.org site. Users are encouraged to affix these Semapedia Tags, which contain embedded Wikipedia URLs, to objects and places in the physical world.

Figure 10.2 A New York Yankees Semapedia Tag.

Figure 10.3 A Semapedia Tag in Jordan.

These Semapedia Tags are mobile-phone-readable physical hyperlinks to the free online encyclopedia Wikipedia. Once the Semapedia Tags are affixed to an object or place in the physical world, anyone with a mobile device with the appropriate 2D barcode reader can access the information that is hyperlinked in the Semapedia Tag. Since the site's launch in 2005, Semapedia Tags have spread on a global scale. See **Figure 10.3**.

Figure 10.4 A Video Meets Function Tag.

Another example of the work that Stan has done with hyperlinking the physical world with the virtual world is his project Video Meets Function (see **Figure 10.4**), which is described as "Places playing Video" where users can connect YouTube videos with a place or thing in the physical world. The Video Meets Function service works by users first searching for a YouTube video on the Video Meets Function site. Once the video is found, users can create a flyer for the video of their choice directly from the site. Users can then print the flyer and then tag it to a corresponding place in the physical world to connect it with the corresponding YouTube video (http://videomeetsfunction.com/).

Interview

AUTHORS: How long have you worked in mobile and what was your first mobile project?

SW: Since 2000. My first project was building the WAP site for IBM wireless. We created that WAP site as an adaptable site that detected user agents, which allowed us to reformat content for different devices like Nokias and BlackBerries.

AUTHORS: Your company, Brothers of Invention, bills itself as an agency that establishes connections between the real-world and mobile Internet services. Tell us about your projects in this space.

SW: There is an obvious need to connect an object with knowledge. It's really not just about a location with knowledge, it's broader. It's about connecting objects with the Internet. From my experience, connecting objects with knowledge is a very natural desire across multiple age groups. If someone is 70 years old or 7 years old, they both would have the same desire to acquire more information about an object that they would hold in their hand.

It's been a very creative time for us right now because we actually have budget to work on interesting projects. In Germany, we're currently working on an RFID project with an urban information system that stretches over hundreds of kilometers. There are RFID beacons along this stretch, where anyone can embed knowledge in these RFID beacons.

AUTHORS: Adoption of 2D barcodes has been rather low in the United States. What do you think are the obstacles that are preventing increased future adoption of 2D barcodes?

SW: There's definitely a mental barrier. A lot of potential users are stuck in the "chicken-and-egg," paradox, and they are waiting for 2D barcodes to instantly take off before they use it, and that will never happen. It's growing slow and if users keep waiting for that fast growth spurt, then nothing will ever happen. This is particularly the case in the United States. Everyone is waiting for that fast growth spurt, and I don't think that will ever happen. My guess is that 2D barcodes will continue to grow slowly, and then one day, it will reach a threshold where the technology then becomes widely available.

AUTHORS: Is there a 2D barcodes standard that you prefer over the others? Additionally, there are image-recognition mobile services like Snaptell and Mobot that also create physical-to-virtual connections. Why do you prefer 2D barcodes over image recognition?

SW: They are two totally different approaches.

The 2D barcodes approach is decentralized because the URL and information are embedded in the 2D barcodes. There is no more routing of information required.

In the case of image-recognition mobile services, you need a resolving server with a database of images, and when you send the server an image, the image will be matched against the database and then resolved to a URL. In my opinion, this type of technology would only be desirable in a closed environment. The image recognition technology works well, but really only in a closed environment—for example, like in a magazine or in conference materials where you can predetermine what images must be in the database. However, if you utilize the technology in an open environment, then there is a good chance that a user can send an image to the server, and that image will be unrecognizable by the system. Once an image is unrecognizable by the system, then you have a situation where the user is getting error message upon error message, which is obviously not a good user experience. This is the biggest issue for me in relation to image-recognition software.

AUTHORS: What are you excited about these days with regards to the mobile industry?

SW: The iPhone. Both the 3G and non-3G versions. I've developed lots of software for mobile phones in the past few years. For me it's the only environment that has industry-standard development tools. Nokia, Ericsson, and Brew: They all require you to purchase expensive licenses to develop. There is a big hurdle to get to a point where you are developing software. Apple recognized that, and they are making it so simple for developers to develop. Also, there is an easy distribution model through the App Store on iTunes. For Nokia, Ericsson, and the other handset manufacturers, it is very difficult to deploy applications because there is no desktop software like iTunes that allows users to easily install applications, and to browse and find applications.

AUTHORS: There are a lot of mobile industry prognosticators saying that 2008 is year of mobile? Do you believe it, or is it yet another false alarm?

SW: I don't quite understand that question. Mobile is already here. The mobile industry may have not manifesed itself in a big bang way, but it's been a slow evolution dating back six years. Text messaging has been pervasive for years. Mobile applications have been pervasive for over five years. Almost every mobile phone has some form of mobile application already installed on it. If you think about it, everyone is using mobile devices now and using them everyday.

I think we have false expectations. Is the industry looking for that big industry mobile-marketing campaign or that killer device like the iPhone? Industry prognosticators are hesitant to call it the year of mobile because no one has created a sustainable advertising model for mobile. But in reality, we have been mobile for years.

With regards to advertising and marketing, the mobile device is such a personal device that I would imagine most users not wanting any advertising on their devices. It is very annoying and offensive to have advertising disturb my flow. That would have a negative impact on me for sure. Mobile devices are very modal, so it's very difficult for a user to avoid advertising. I would try my best to avoid advertising on my mobile device.

AUTHORS: You have spent time in Asia and Europe in recent years. What are some mobile user behaviors over there that you could envision becoming adopted in the United States?

SW: In Hong Kong, the Near Field Communications (NFC) mobile applications are very advanced. In the convenience stores over there, people are paying for goods using their NFC-enabled mobile devices. NFC mobile payments are quite pervasive in Asia. Right now, there are only NFC mobile payment trials happening in some select neighborhoods, but I could imagine NFC-based mobile wallets being adopted in the U.S. on a mass scale, especially in the larger urban areas like New York.

I also could imagine data access on the trains being pervasive in the U.S. at some point in the future. In most Asian cities, you can text and browse the mobile web while sitting on the train.

AUTHORS: Any last words of inspiration for the creatives, designers, and developers working in the mobile industry?

SW: Always use open technologies, never use closed technologies. When you use open technologies, you are going to be able to multiply the adoption of your software. That is the only way to go. It's a very easy way for people to develop additional applications on open technologies, and it doesn't require you to buy a license. There are so many open technologies out there, you can build anything you can imagine.

11

Urban Navigation Service

Name: Michael Sharon

Occupation: CTO, Founder of Socialight

Device: Uses the original iPhone and an N95 8GB

Mobile Data Habits: Consumes mobile content multiple times an hour. Plays mobile games whenever he's got free time in the subway.

Background

Michael Sharon is a media artist, writer, and programmer whose work runs the gamut from mobile social software to gestural music interfaces to big games and everything in between. He is also an adjunct professor at New York University's Interactive Telecommunications Program. Michael's work has been featured in a number of outlets, including *The Wall Street Journal*, The Discovery Channel, *The New York Times*, *Wired*, *The Guardian*, and *The London Times*, among others. **FIGURE 11.1** shows the Socialight home page. **Figure 11.2** provides a glimpse of how Socialight works.

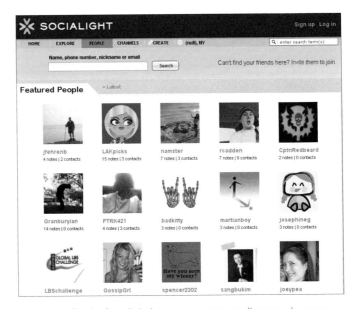

FIGURE 11.1 On the Socialight home page, you can discover places on your mobile device and share them with friends.

FIGURE 11.2 Connecting with people in Socialight.

Interview

AUTHORS: How long have you worked in mobile, and what was your first mobile project?

MS: I've worked in mobile on and off for the last four years, but I cut my teeth working on a project in South Africa in 2001. I was working for this small, interactive shop that put together a mobile gambling promotion for an online gambling site. It was a simple version of roulette using SMS—just send in an SMS and you've placed a bet on red or black with the chance to win real money. I've heard rumors that this won't work very well in the U.S.

AUTHORS: Tell us a bit about your company, Socialight, which is described as a social mapping service that allows users to append text, images, audio, and video to any physical location. How does the service work? Is it utilizing GPS? Cell triangulation? Mobile site? Mobile application? Web site? Where is the service currently available?

MS: Socialight is an urban navigation service focused on helping people discover relevant local content. Socialight's mobile community platform unlocks the ability for people to find recommendations and stories about places around them from friends and trusted brands. We use people's locations, interests, and social networks to serve up the most interesting information to any person at any particular moment, allowing them to tap into the local buzz right from their cell phones. We originally used GPS to enable precise location tracking with a "personal radar" type service, but we quickly realized that the value proposition was applicable to many more devices using far rougher location estimation, so we ported the original client to a number of other platforms. Users' locations are determined using any available source, including GPS, TDOA, Geo IP, WiFi positioning, and direct geocoding. As a result, Socialight can be accessed on almost any mobile network in the world. Today, Socialight is available through the web, mobile web, and SMS, as well as Java and native iPhone clients.

AUTHORS: In your opinion, where is GPS heading within mobile, and how valuable is GPS to a consumer's experience while using mobile services? Do you think consumers have been quick to adopt or demand GPS-based mobile services and applications?

MS: I think GPS and LBS in particular have become confusingly intertwined with each other and are used metonymically to refer to the broad capability of location in mobile applications. Nobody wakes up in the morning eager to get a fix of Location-Based Services or some Global Positioning System. It's the capacity and capability to add location to applications like search, SMS, browsing, and social networking that make people sit up and pay attention.

When applications add location and are able to easily close the loop and deliver dramatic improvements in user experience as a result—it educates consumers about what to expect from location services, as well as raises the bar for developers. One example that springs to mind here is Google's MyLocation feature, which used cell tower positioning to rapidly provide a rough estimate of location for almost any user—which in turn led to the consumer being educated about the benefits of control-plane-positioning technology, in a way they could quickly grasp.

The mainstream consumer has not been quick to adopt GPS-based mobile services or applications, apart from search and navigation applications such as VZ Navigator, Google Maps Mobile, and the Maps application on the iPhone. Beyond the core navigation and search categories, up until now, there have been very few applications that have caught the consumer's imagination and become mainstream successes. The difficulty has always been the number of pieces required to success-fully deliver a location-enabled service, with user experience always suffering due to distribution, technology, or some other element that couldn't be successfully massaged. In addition, the number of devices and networks that supported location services has also been a minority until now.

The iPhone's App Store and Apple's Cocoa Touch Location APIs are game-changers in the sense that they solve two of the most challenging issues for developers: distribution and technical difficulty. This combination has made it simple to create basic "check-in" style, location-enabled apps such as Loopt, Whrrl, or Platial's Nearby. More complex behavior that requires passive location tracking cannot be accomplished at this stage, and as of now (September 2008), mainstream con-sumer adoption still remains somewhat elusive.

AUTHORS: Currently, all of the big web-based social networks like Facebook, MySpace, and Friendster have all extended their service offerings to the mobile medium. However, there are several mobile-only social networks out there like Zannel and itsmy.com. In your opinion, why would consumers decide to use a mobile-only social network versus just extending their current usage of a web-based social network to mobile? Are there features that mobile-only social networks provide that are advantageous to the big web-based social networks?

MS: I think the only advantage of using a mobile-only social network is for people that don't have access to a full web device—in those cases, using mobile-only social networks may be more useful than a web-based social network, which requires that you sign up and access the service at least part of the time on the full web. I think easy mobile signup is probably the number-one feature that mobile-only networks have that web-based social networks need to integrate more effectively.

AUTHORS: Let's talk about your experience teaching at NYU ITP for a second. It's a known fact that the digital/interactive/mobile industries are currently experiencing a huge talent shortage, thus highlighting the need to train the next generation of thinkers, designers, and developers at the university/graduate school level. In your opinion, what are some of the top university programs that are training the next generation of mobile designers and programmers? What are some of the core fundamental principles around mobile that you try to instill in your students?

MS: There are some great programs out there training future generations of mobile creative, and we're really starting to see many more people take an interest in developing for device platforms with the largest installed base in the world (theoretically!). I think the top university programs for nurturing mobile talent include schools with traditionally strong engineering departments, such as MIT, Stanford, and Carnegie Mellon, as well as design programs such as ITP, Parsons, and RCA.

One of the core principles that I try to convey to the students in my mobile class is to maintain a high degree of user and context-awareness—to ensure that they craft the features and UI of the application or service they're designing by taking the needs and constraints of their intended users into account. Once they've created a product that fulfills a specific user need, then they refine and iterate using principles such as:

1 Reduce transaction costs (wherever possible).

2 Display the most relevant information immediately.

3 Use lowest-common-denominator technology (if possible).

AUTHORS: In your mind, what's the most inspirational thing happening in the mobile world these days? GPS? Application explosion? Better devices? Renewed consumer appetite for mobile data services?

MS: Discovery. Apple nailed the mobile distribution channel with their App Store, solving many of the problems that caused mobile developers to beat their heads against the wall in frustration for years. Over 100 million applications have been downloaded to just a few million phones in a matter of months. More importantly, these applications were released by a wide range of developers without requiring deals with carriers. Although mobile application portals like Handango or GetJar have been around for a number of years, Apple's vertically integrated App Store clearly showed users the value proposition with a very well thought out experience. This is an area that will see a flurry of development in the next few months, as competitors such as Nokia's MOSH and Google's Android Marketplace try to duplicate Apple's success.

AUTHORS: Fast-forward five years into the future: Can you paint me a picture of the mobile world?

MS: I hate making predictions. It's nearly impossible to get them right, and many smarter people than me have been famously wrong over and over again ("640K should be enough for anyone?" "There is a worldwide market for maybe five computers?"). That said, since you asked, I'm going to take a quick stream-of-consciousness stab in a few directions that I think mobile is going. Anyone waking up five years from now will find themselves in a very different mobile world— features found in the smartphones of today will be de rigeur for entry-level devices that are given away by the carriers. Smartphones at that stage will include location (indoor, outdoor), RFID readers and digital compasses, and will be widely used as general-purpose computing, identification, payment, and navigation devices, as well as communication tools. The carriers themselves have finally woken up and realized that they are not the all-singing, all-dancing media and content companies that they wanted to be, and have focused on their core competencies—providing solid voice-and-data services on great devices. They are pipes, but these are proud pipes. Developers will still be living in a world of fragmentation, but a number of tools will have emerged to allow for rapid development of applications based on familiar design patterns. Open source software will enjoy a tremendous reach in this world, both on the handset and the tools side, but numerous proprietary OSs and toolkits will remain. Application discovery will be far easier than it is today, but finding the best applications will still rely on word of mouth.

AUTHORS: Any last words of inspiration for the creatives, designers, and developers working in the mobile industry?

MS: Whatever you're building, put the user first. If you can capture their desires, meet their needs, and ease some frustrations—then your application has a much better chance of breaking through the clutter and actually being used.

12

Mobile in Academia

Name: Shawn Van Every

Occupation: Professor, New York University, Interactive Telecommunications Program

Device: Currently uses a Nokia N95 (8GB U.S. 3G version) for voice, SMS, MMS, photos, videos, and sometimes data (generally apps for photo/video upload).

Mobile Data Habits: Uses SMS/MMS a couple of times a day. Uses an iPhone (version 1) for utilizing the web and other applications (mainly email) very, very often (all day if not at his computer). Uses maps, Facebook, Twitter, video consuming, and a couple of other applications on an irregular basis.

Background

Shawn is a teacher in NYU's Interactive Telecommunications Program. His academic research focus is on emerging technologies related to media creation, distribution, and interaction. His projects generally involve development of tools that help to make low cost media making, distribution, and interactivity possible. Specifically he works with online audio/video and mobile devices.

His teaching is varied and includes courses on participatory and social media, programming, mobile technologies, and interactive telephony.

Recently Shawn was honored with the David Payne Carter award for excellence in teaching. He has demonstrated, exhibited, and presented work at many conferences and technology demonstrations, including O'Reilly's Emerging Telephony, O'Reilly's Emerging Technology, ACM Multimedia, Vloggercon, and Strong Angel II. He was a co-organizer of the Open Media Developers Summit, Beyond Broadcast (2006), and iPhoneDev-Camp NYC.

Interview

AUTHORS: Tell us about the class that you teach and any mobile projects that you have recently worked on.

SVE: I teach a couple of classes that relate to mobile:

The first is called "Mobile Me(dia)." First of all, I should explain the name. "Me" refers to the fact that the mobile device is a very personal communication device and in many cases is used for purposes of self-identification and self-expression (ringtones and so on). It is also the device that people would choose to give up last, as it is so pivotal to their daily lives.

The second part of "Media" is an exploration of the device as a media creation, sharing, and consumption device. The mobile phone—always on, always connected with great media creation capabilities—is ripe for activities such as are happening on the Internet with media creation, sharing, and consuming. In the class we investigate how to connect the pieces and talk a lot about the implications of such.

Another course that I teach is called "Redial: Interactive Telephony." In that course, we explored the traditional use of the telephone as a one-to-one communications device through voice and Touch-Tone. We utilize (and abuse) an open source PBX system called Asterisk. Through the course, students learn how the PSTN and VoIP systems work, and how they can both be utilized through Asterisk to do anything from create interesting find-me follow-me applications, new takes on voice mail combined with things like podcasting or used to interact or control any networked device such as a screen running Flash or a physical object with an Arduino.

Interestingly enough, the "Redial" course is extremely popular, more popular than the "Mobile Me(dia)" course. I believe this is due to the fact that the first and foremost capability of the mobile phone is making phone calls, and this is universal through demographics such as age, sex, income, and so forth. One-hundred percent of mobile users worldwide use their phones to make calls, whereas only 50 percent or so do something as advanced as SMS messaging. Easily bringing the normal phone call into the realm of interactive media is incredibly appealing.

AUTHORS: What are some of the notable mobile projects (commercial, art, or academic) that you have been a fan of over the last few years?

SVE: There are quite a few that I am very fond of for various reasons. I'll start with the earliest and go from there:

DIALATONES (A TELESYMPHONY) BY GOLAN LEVIN ET AL. (2001)

 www.flong.com/projects/telesymphony/

This project utilized the ringtone functionality of mobile phones in the possession of audience members to assist in the production of a musical piece. Different groups of audience members were given ringtones and were called throughout the piece.

While I didn't witness this directly, I have seen some video and talked with one of the collaborators (Greg Shakar), and I think it is marvelous!

 Dodgeball: www.dodgeball.com (2004)

Dodgeball is location-based mobile social software that simply uses SMS messaging. Prior to Dodgeball, all of the location-based mobile social software I saw attempted to work through an installed application, which significantly reduced the number of people who would or could participate (data plans and GPS-enabled devices). Using SMS as the means to "check-in" and tell the system where you are was brilliant and shows what can be done with such simple technology. No need to have the system do the parts that it can't do when it is easy to just ask the user.

MOBILE PROCESSING

I have been teaching processing as an introductory tool for a few years. It works very well as an intro tool and is especially valuable since students learn to program in Java and get visual results immediately (this would take at least an entire semester to cover in straight Java).

Bringing this tool to the mobile realm offers some of the same advantages and is a perfect starting point for application development in J2ME on the mobile phone. It is fun, consistent (even when the handsets aren't), somewhat easy, and extensible. Furthermore it is open source.

PYTHON S60

While I am not a fan of Python, I am a big fan of Python for S60 devices. There is one main reason: It shows the power and creativity of what can be done on the device when programming is done in an easy-to-use open language that exposes all of the features and functionality of the phone. JME has been locked down on mobile devices in so many ways that it is often frustrating to get what you want to work, and C++ is just plain too hard for most of my students.

IPHONE

Finally phones that are useable and have a modern operating system. (I don't feel the need to expound on this, as so many people have already in the past, and it just gets boring.)

LINUX, OPENMOKO, AND ESPECIALLY ANDROID

Finally, phones that are open! Let the fun begin!

WEBKIT

A great open source mobile browser that acts like a desktop browser and is installed on a bunch of devices already: S60, Android, iPhone.

AUTHORS: The mobile world is definitely growing fast these days and there are lots of areas within mobile that a student could choose from, such as SMS, mobile site builds, application development, IVR systems, location-based, and mobile social networking. In your opinion, which areas do you see as being the most popular with students these days?

SVE: In my experience IVR systems, as evidenced by my "Redial" class, followed by application development (spurred on by the iPhone), with location-based and social being in the mix. SMS is definitely widely used but generally in the context of other services such as Twitter. I haven't seen anyone build a decent mobile site for a project in a while; I think it is a given to the students that mobile browsers are starting to act like desktop browsers therefore no need to deal with .mobi/WAP/XHTML for mobile. I also think that, given that navigation to a particular site is difficult on the mobile, specific mobile sites aren't that likely to garner much traffic.

AUTHORS: In your mind, what are the hottest areas of mobile right now? Location-based applications? New interfaces? Better devices? Renewed consumer uptake for mobile data services?

SVE: This is snarky, but easy access to the Internet through mobile devices is probably the hottest technology. Of course, better interfaces (iPhone in particular), better devices with more capabilities are great, but simply faster and more reliable Internet access is what I feel is driving interesting development.

AUTHORS: In what areas is the academic world currently lacking when it comes to teaching the next generation of mobile thinkers, designers, and developers?

SVE: Open access to the networks: The high cost of data services, the limited ability to deploy applications in the wild, and locked-down development platforms are really a big problem for students with big ideas.

AUTHORS: It's a known fact that the digital/interactive/mobile industries are currently experiencing a huge talent shortage, thus highlighting the need to train the next generation of thinkers, designers, and developers at the university/graduate school level. In your opinion, what are some of the top university programs that are training the next generation of mobile designers and programmers? What are some of the core fundamental principles around mobile that you try to instill in your students?

SVE: ITP/NYU. The normal group: MIT, CMU, and the like....

One that many people have probably not heard of is Lancaster University's Infolab21 in the UK. Dr. Paul Coulton and his students are creating excellent mobile applications, games, and really pushing things.

 www.infolab21.lancs.ac.uk/news_and_events/news/?article_id=525

Principles: These devices aren't about consumption. They aren't televisions. Their original purpose is as a two-way communications device. Keep that in mind.

Other than that, I talk about things such as existing services and not having to build everything from scratch, doing quick prototypes in Java/Flash, and release early, release often.

AUTHORS: Fast-forward five years into the future. Can you paint us picture of the mobile world?

SVE: I am going to beg out of this one and instead paint a picture of my utopia:

Five years from now: Carriers have accepted the fact that they are too large and slow to beat the current crop of DIY wireless systems that are being built and increasingly being used. They have realized that the cost of maintaining service such as the little-used voice platform is not worthwhile when all that anyone cares about is the openness and speed of their Internet connections. Besides, they are sick of battling the hackers, who continually figure out how to bypass their restrictions, and really sick of spending their lobbying money to battle Googlezon and the like over whether or not they have to carry their data without charge.

They have finally realized and accepted their place in the world as "dumb pipes," wireless ISPs.

They have given up on locking down phones. Nobody will sign a two-year contract anymore for a free phone that they can't install any of the open source software on.

On the other side of the coin, Googlezon, DIYers, hackers, and hipsters are developing and deploying game-changing hardware and applications at a phenomenal pace. A prolific open source community has introduced a kit-based mobile phone with every feature imaginable and battery life that puts devices from five years ago to shame. Tourists are carrying around monstrous-looking, home-built teleconferencing systems with them as they gawk at the Naked Cowboy in Times Square and talk with their relatives and friends back home. Hipsters in Bushwick no longer carry laptops and projectors to their VJ gigs, but rather bring their mobile-projector-enabled, high-speed, wireless video-mixing systems, and no longer have to be hunched over a keyboard and mouse. They simply mingle with the crowd or dance until they drop, with every movement being tracked by sensors programmed to project and mix particular clips or dynamically generated visuals.

I can't think of anyone who uses a laptop computer anymore. Everyone seems to have adopted the projected keyboard and gesture-controlled interfaces that are common on mobile devices now.

Data flows pretty seamlessly, and just by pointing to a contact in the sky, a voice, data, or text channel is opened to that person.

Wow... Things are different now that the networks have been broken.

AUTHORS: Any last words of inspiration for the creatives, designers, and developers working in the mobile industry?

SVE: This is just beginning. The technology being developed will need your ideas, big and small, for a long time to come. You are in a position to create the next generation of applications that will be usable by billions of people worldwide.

13

Mobile in Art

Name: Carlos Gomez de Llarena

Occupation: Media Architect, Digital Artist

Device: iPhone 2.5G version

Mobile Data Habits: Checks mobile content more than 10 times a day, probably throughout the day. Performs a mix of checking email, weather, and subway maps, among other things.

Background

Carlos is a media architect engaged in the design of the digital media that shapes our newly found perceptions of space and social interaction.

He works with a diverse palette of tools, including installation, video, sound, wireless networks, the web, and programming. His work has been shown at Ars Electronica, Eyebeam, the Museum of Contemporary Art of Caracas, ZKM, ResFest, and the Seoul Net Festival, among others. His background is in architecture, video, and interactive media. He currently lives in New York, where he works as a freelance interaction designer and developer of media architecture hybrids.

In September 2003, the Ars Electronica Prix honored one of his wireless projects, Node Runner, with the Golden Nica for Net Vision. He also performs as a VJ in his spare time and has done visuals in Caracas and New York City for raves and celebrity DJs.

Interview

AUTHORS: How long have you worked in mobile, and what was your first mobile project?

CG: I've been working with mobile technologies and concepts pretty much since I was at NYU ITP in 2000. Starting in the year 2000, I was only thinking about theoretical future interactions with mobile devices, but not really building much with them. In the second year I did get a lot more hands-on with WiFi, which was starting to become a little bit more available in 2002 so I … I think my first mobile project was using WiFi and was actually a part of my thesis project at ITP. I did a program that was actually a very broad exploration about the future of interactive television programming, but not using set-box solutions that were interactive, but rather combining normal TV transmission with online networks and mobile devices to sort of create a feedback loop between networks and users.

The idea was called Remote Control Citizen, and the idea was to use a WiFi-enabled laptop with a webcam attached to it streaming a live show on the streets of New York. It was about discovering neighborhoods in New York. So I did a pilot project in Tompkins Square Park, and I had a web page at ITP that was being displayed on a big plasma screen and people were actually seeing my live webcam streamed from Tompkins Square on the web site, I also had a small form on the site that allowed users to send me a text message while I was in Tompkins Square with questions that people wanted me to ask to people that I ran into on the street.

AUTHORS: You have a very unique background when it comes to mobile. Not only have you been working on commercial mobile products for a few years; you've also worked on a number of mobile art projects dating back to 2000. Tell us about how you balance working across both commercial projects and art projects, and whether or not the two feed into each other.

CG: I would say absolutely it's all part of my own, like, brainstorming process. A lot of ideas that I think are appropriate for a client actually might have something to do with an idea that I thought of for an art project and vice versa. I think it's sort of very symbiotic at that point how the ideas form and as for trying to keep a balance, that is actually one of the things that I've had to struggle with the most with because commercial work as we all know is very demanding and challenging, and I'm very engaged by those challenges, but it is also very much consuming of all my energy, so at some points in my recent career, I've had to postpone a lot of the artwork that I've been meaning to do. Projects that I thought would take me a certain amount of time ended up spiraling out of control in terms of schedule, and that's something that really frustrates me, but I've always tried to persevere to the commitment and get to finish the project, even if it takes me more time due to commercial demands. I'm very much inspired by both commercial- and art-based mobile projects. I've been fortunate enough to get to work on very cool commercial mobile projects, and certainly the art side is also the case.

When I first discovered QR Codes, I was doing a lot of research around commercial applications of it. I was thinking primarily of QR Codes in terms of applications for marketing. It was hard to do a lot of those QR Code projects with clients because the QR Codes were sort of ahead of their time in a way, and a lot of those ideas we had about using QR Codes on physical environments had to be postponed. Where I did get to work with QR Codes was on one of my more recent outdoor installations, the Fulton Fence project. See **FIGURE 13.1** and **FIGURE 13.2**. We did get to use the codes in a very sort of artistic way that made sense with the whole concept of the installation.

[The Fulton Fence was a temporary installation in Fulton Street, New York City on view from November 14, 2007, through the spring of 2008. The project was a response to the effects of development—in particular the visual pollution created by the presence of construction sites in a small, concentrated area. This web site, www.fultonfence.net/, parallels the physical intervention in lower Manhattan, and explores the notion of "site" as both location and information.]

FIGURE 13.1 The Houston Street "sister" fence next to the Fulton Fence.

FIGURE 13.2 Capturing a QR Code on the fence.

AUTHORS: Tell us about your Urballoon project and/or any other mobile art projects that you have worked on.

CG: The Urballoon project was one of those projects that was pretty inspiring for me when I came up with the idea. But I had a lot of struggle, and I actually still do with it in some other ways. I had to struggle a lot in terms of getting to produce it, actually. It was a project that I proposed as part of a residency at Eyebeam, and it was actually, you know, those residencies were, like, six months long. And I had put together a timeline and budget to do it, and obviously there was almost no money for that project when I got the residency.

But the worst part of it was getting to actually devote time to the research and build all the different pieces. The main idea of that project is an urban media space enabled by wireless technologies, so it's a big 10-foot balloon with a video projector and a WiFi laptop that allows people to submit content via a web site or a mobile device connected to the web site. These images and texts can get projected wherever the balloon actually is. See Figure 13.3 and Figure 13.4. The balloon itself has a big URL of the project, urballoon.com, on the side of it as it hovers on top of the street. I get a lot of online participation and, you know, physical participation from people on the street when they see the project. It's been a lot of fun. I've also been applying for a patent for this project over the last three years now, and it's been its own sort of process to deal with, and I had an opportunity to do it commercially for a client, and that was more challenging than I would have expected, and it made me realize that the balloon has some design flaws, in terms of the actual installation, that I need to address. Depending upon the weather conditions, it becomes a little bit unstable when there are winds of a certain strength. Urballoon has been one of those really long projects that I've consistently been working on.

FIGURE 13.3 Urballoon floating in the sky, waiting to project down onto the world.

FIGURE 13.4 Urballoon in action, projecting images and text down onto the world.

Some other art projects, I think it's more of a service, but it's definitely more of a service. It's not art. It's this MetropoliPhone web site I built recently for the iPhone. It's simply a collection of subway maps and public transportation maps, including buses and ferries and tramways of cities from all over the world. See **Figure 13.5**. It's just a list that you scroll, then you open it to the intuitive interactions of the iPhone, and it becomes actually a very useful thing to have with you when you need a quick reference of the metropolitan transportation resource.

Figure 13.5 MetropoliPhone is a collection of handy city maps.

AUTHORS: Your Urballoon project is about creating an urban media space with a floating balloon that is constantly connected to a WiFi connection. With total WiMAX connectivity on the horizon, and 3G cellular networks a reality, paint us a picture of what you imagine the future of the urban mobile landscape will be. Will all objects be networked? Will objects communicate with humans and vice versa?

CG: Definitely I think all objects being networked is certainly a trend that we're starting to see already available. I have been following a lot about the ZigBee protocol and also RFID applications. I think the type of scenarios that I'm envisioning right now are almost clichés because futurists have already been talking about these scenarios for years. I think that one thing that might start happening is the fact that objects are being networked, and how the networks will begin to behave. I have been thinking about networks that might actually never be connected to the web, but rather networks that are very localized between objects that serve specific purposes, which might not even require sharing any type of information data.

Examples of this would be mass networks that ZigBee devices might track, a particular sort of network of objects or spaces in a city. For example, if we think about this in the context of games. If we have a game where people have ZigBee-enabled shoes or wristbands that as they're walking by, or running by ZigBee-enabled game pieces on the city or buildings, then all sorts of interactions and experiences would start happening. These networks I think are going to be extremely tactical and reconfigurable, and easy to mount and dismount.

AUTHORS: What are some of the notable mobile art projects that you have been a fan of over the last few years?

CG: I love the guerilla SMS projector by Troika. It reminds me a lot of Urballoon, too. I just like the "guerilla-ness" of it.

I also liked some of the stuff that AreaCode has been doing, too. I remember reading about a game they were developing for a Japanese company that would use a new sort of evolved version of GPS sensor tied to an accelorametor, so that the phone could actually understand not only where you were, but also where your phone was pointing to and at what height, so it could like read the azimuth level of your tilt. It could even understand that you were pointing at the penthouse of the Empire State Building versus pointing at the ground level. I don't know if they actually got to build it—it just sounded like some sick technology and possibly a sick game, too.

AUTHORS: Let's circle back to the commercial side of things for a second. Mobile web usage is up to almost 19 percent (up from 12 percent last year), and the iPhone App Store has registered 60 million downloads since it opened on July 11th, 2008. Do you think the mobile industry is finally starting to enter its golden age? What would you like to see from the commercial side of things for the mobile industry? Better content? New interfaces? More GPS-based apps?

CG: I think it is probably the dawn of the golden age. I think the actual best of it is still a few years away. I think the iPhone has done a tremendous job of getting it right. I think they didn't necessarily reinvent completely what the phone is but rather how we're supposed to use it and experience it. I think that the real innovations here are in user experience. A lot of the stuff they have there, I think we've seen a lot of those ideas being tried out by so many companies before, but with mixed degrees of success. So I think that particular innovation of getting it right and sort of subtracting the sort of unnecessary stuff in order to get it right, that is going to usher a lot of, you know, responses from the rest of the industry.

I think we still need to give it a few more cycles to get it right. Of course the numbers are going to keep going up in terms of adoption and ideas and innovation. But I think in order to get to the most shockingly futuristic applications, we really need the ridiculous networks of the future to be deployed, such as WiMAX, LTE, ZigBee, and RFID. That's why I think we're still a few more years away, because the infrastructure networks are currently being deployed, and they won't be covering the whole U.S. or the whole world until a few years later.

Also, the products that get the experience right are going to take probably similar time frames to start emerging. And once we get those products out, I think we're going to start to see even more radically new experiences of how all these objects kind of relate with each other.

AUTHORS: Are there any commercial mobile projects these days that are really inspiring you? It could be anything from a project to a technology to a device.

CG: I'm certainly attracted to WiMAX's technology, but I think ... I worry that it is sort of already obsolete when it hasn't even been deployed because I've been reading a lot of criticism about it, and most of the industry moving toward LTE. I do think it still holds a lot of promise for the rest of the world, so to speak.

AUTHORS: When you're going about your art projects, are you actually keeping in mind target audiences, or are you doing more of a general approach toward hitting the highest common denominator of handsets. I mean is there a certain methodology that you've been using for your art projects?

CG: That's an excellent question. I've been trying to push the envelope on those projects and at the same time I'm very aware that people don't carry with them a lot of the technologies that my projects may require. What I've been trying to do is provide alternate entry points to the experience, if they happen to not have those key technologies or software that are required.

However, for the Fulton Fence QR Code project, almost nobody had QR Code readers on their mobile devices, but that project was more of a highbrow idea, sort of more future looking. But we also did show the URL of the web site that the code pointed to, and we had it printed out right next to the code pretty legibly, so people could also understand that there is a web site that has some information. We weren't really explaining any more than that. And I think that was sort of the entry point to show the URL with a code.

AUTHORS: Any last words of inspiration for the creatives, designers, and developers working in the mobile industry?

CG: I'm actually excited to see what sort of design and ideas will be explored. I have a lot of respect for other people working in the field. I'm inspired by it myself. In general I have one word of advice: I think there's a concerning trend that we as a culture are getting seduced too much by the possibilities of technology—and this overdriving of more information and web services. And what I'm noticing is that a lot of the stuff is technically cool, but I worry that it is adding a lot of noise to the way we live our lives. Like I don't think I need 35 different location-based social networks on my device.

I worry that we're going to spend too much of our lives in a sort of mediated screen mode, and we might lose something that was really important all along in terms of just being here with people around you, and not sort of being constantly out there on that screen with Facebook or some LBS application. I would like for designers and technologists to find a homeostasis, a kind of balance for life.

Index

A

accessibility, mobile medium design challenges, 8

advertising
  bringing traditional static to life, 51–53
  engaging users, 18
  global mobile, 38–39
  OOH (Out of Home)
    Bluetooth and WiFi casting, 71–72
    2D barcodes, 73–74
    Interactive Voice Response (IVR), 72–73
    mobile Internet for print, 74
    SMS, 69–71

Amazon, TextBuyIt, 58

Americas, global community differences, 26–27

Android, native application development, 124

AOL iPhone Music App, 58–59

Applets, user quality assurance, 100

applications
  development for global mobile, 23–24
  downloadable, 13

art (digital), Llarena, Carols Gomez de
  background, 192
  interview, 192–202

Asia Pacific, global community differences, 27–32

author's interviews
  Becker, Michael, 152–157
  Every, Shawn Van, 185–190
  Llarena, Carols Gomez de, 192–202

Muller, Alex, 161–166
Sharon, Michael, 177–182
Wiechers, Stan, 170–173

B

Ballard, Barbara, *Designing the Mobile User Experience*, 105, 112

banner units, mobile to mobile communications, 63–64

Becker, Michael
  author interview, 152–157
  background, 150–152

billboards
  controlling with mobile, 50–51
  text-message-enabling, 50

Bluecasting
  engaging users, 17
  progressive mobile medium, 51

Bluetooth
  print to mobile communications, 71–72
  user quality assurance, 101

brick cell phone, 42

broadcast to mobile communications, 75–76
  mobile Internet, 76–77
  SMS, 77–78
  third-party services, 78–79

Brothers of Invention, LLC, 168–173

browsing, subscriber growth, 6

C

China, global community differences, 30–31

color optimization, visual design, 130–131

Europe, Middle East, and Africa (EMEA), global community differences, 32–33

Every, Shawn Van
background, 184
interview, 185–190

F–G

Flash Lite, mobile game, 14

flat-rate data plans, 23

focus groups, testing prototypes, 120–121

global mobile
advertising, 38–39
developing strategy
design for audience, 36
establish architecture and development, 35
gathering research and statistics, 34–35
manage messaging components, 37
manage regional costs, 38
rigorous quality assurance processes, 36–37
Internet growth, 22–24
media content, 39–40
regional differences, 25
Americas, 26–27
Asia Pacific, 27–32
EMEA (Europe, Middle East, and Africa), 32–33
3G growth, 24–25

Google Android, native application development, 124

Google SMS, 57

GSM, 22

H–I

handsets
manufacturer development, 23
users, 87–89

detection, 93–96
testing, 96–98

Hong Kong, global community differences, 31

iLoopMobile, 151–152

India, global community differences, 32

interaction design
Every, Shawn Van
background, 184
interview, 185–190
mobile design process, 111–112
developing designs, 116–120
testing and refining, 120–121
user research, 112–116
resources
mobile web, 123
native application development, 124
SMS, 122–123
small screens, 104–105
capability variation, 108–109
leverage built-in hardware, 110–111
screen size variation, 107–108
user behaviors, 110
user expectations, 109–110
varying input modalities, 105–106

interactive television, 44–45

Interactive Voice Response (IVR), 14–15
communication modes
print to mobile, 72–73
web to mobile, 67–68
user quality assurance, 101–102

Internet, 2–3
communication modes
broadcast to mobile, 76–77
radio to mobile, 80–81
global growth, 22–24
progressive mobile medium, 47–49

iPhone, 106
Digg.com, 109
native application development, 124
Web Development guidelines, 123

IVR (Interactive Voice Response), 14–15
  communication modes
    print to mobile, 72–73
    web to mobile, 67–68
  user quality assurance, 101–102

J–K

L

M